The Church Rocks!

The Church Rocks!

A History of the Catholic Church for Kids and Their Parents and Teachers

Mary Lea Hill, FSP

Pauline
BOOKS & MEDIA
Boston

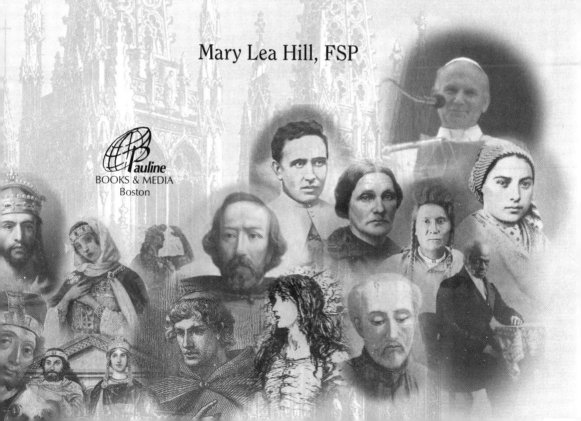

Library of Congress Cataloging-in-Publication Data

Names: Hill, Mary Lea, author.
Title: The church rocks! : a history of the Catholic church for kids and their : parents and teachers / Mary Lea Hill, FSP.
Description: Boston : Pauline Books & Media, [2018] | Audience: Age 9-12. | Audience: Grade 4 to 6.
Identifiers: LCCN 2016058198| ISBN 9780819816573 (pbk.) | ISBN 0819816574 (pbk.)
Subjects: LCSH: Catholic Church--History--Juvenile literature.
Classification: LCC BX948 .H55 2017 | DDC 282.09--dc23
LC record available at https://lccn.loc.gov/2016058198

The Scripture quotations contained herein are from the *New Revised Standard Version Bible: Catholic Edition*, copyright © 1989, 1993, Division of Christian Education of the National Council of the Churches of Christ in the United States of America. Used by permission. All rights reserved.

Design by Mary Joseph Peterson, FSP and Putri Magdalena Mamesah, FSP
Cover design by Mary Joseph Peterson, FSP
Edited by Jaymie Stuart Wolfe and Marlyn Evangelina Monge, FSP

"P" and PAULINE are registered trademarks of the Daughters of St. Paul.

Copyright © 2018, Daughters of St. Paul

Published by Pauline Books & Media, 50 Saint Pauls Avenue, Boston, MA 02130–3491

Printed in the U.S.A.

TCR VSAUSAPEOILL5-1510090 1657-4

www.pauline.org

Pauline Books & Media is the publishing house of the Daughters of St. Paul, an international congregation of women religious serving the Church with the communications media.

1 2 3 4 5 6 7 8 9   22 21 20 19 18

Contents

Visit www.pauline.org/churchrocks
to download the appendices: Table
of Popes, of Church Councils, and of
Heresies

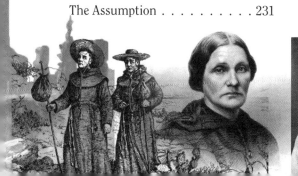

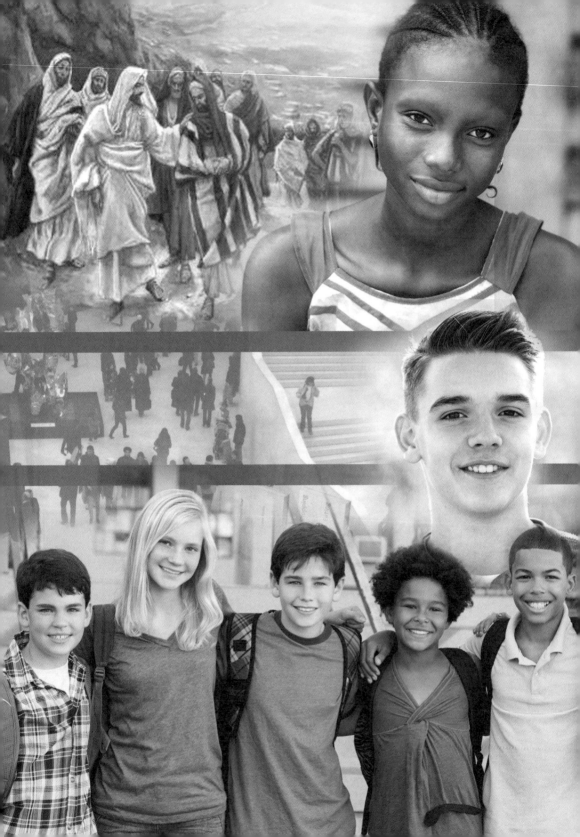

Introduction

You are living history. Everything that happens becomes part of history. Have you read about something or seen a story in the news that you think will become part of our study of history in the future? Just think: when you are grown up you can tell your children, "I was in school when that happened; when that was discovered; when that was invented."

History is the story of people—both individuals and groups of them. Because the Church is the People of God, it also has a story. It is the fascinating journey of Jesus Christ's disciples over a little more than two thousand years. Church history is the true story of our family of faith that leads all the way up to today.

In these pages we will trace the Church's adventure from Pentecost until our own century. As we read, we thank God for the gift of the Church and for all those who make up the Church's story. Along the way we'll discover that it's *our* story— yours and mine—too.

Prologue

10 BC

1 BC — 3 BC or AD 1—Jesus is born.

Basket makers (also known as the *Anasazi*) begin farming settlements in the North American southwest.

AD 1 — AD 1—Judea becomes a Roman province.

AD 15 — AD 14—Emperor Augustus dies after choosing Tiberius as the next emperor.

AD 25 — AD 25—The Eastern Han Dynasty begins in China.

AD 30 or 33—The Death, Resurrection, and Ascension of Jesus take place.

AD 35 — AD 30 or 33—Pentecost.

The Church Is Born

Pentecost

Church of Believers

Jesus ascended into heaven forty days after he rose from the dead. His friends were sad and afraid. They missed being with their Risen Lord. Jesus had appeared to them and spoken with them as naturally as he had always done. Now that Jesus was gone, his disciples hid in the Upper Room. They gathered in the place where he had celebrated his Last Supper with them. Peter, Andrew, James, John, Philip, Bartholomew, Thomas, Matthew, James, Simon, and Jude Thaddeus were there. Matthias also joined them. He had been chosen to take the place of Judas Iscariot, the one who had betrayed Jesus. These apostles were joined by many other disciples of the Lord. Among them were a number of devoted women and Mary, the Mother of Jesus.

Jesus had appeared in that very room after his resurrection, to assure his friends that he was alive again. He had told his followers to preach the Good News of salvation to everyone in the whole world. They were to go out and baptize new believers. The Holy Spirit, Jesus had promised, would be their guide: "He will remind you of all I have said." That promise caused the disciples to wait and pray in the Upper Room. It gave them hope.

"My name is Esther. I listened to Jesus teach many times. He liked having us kids around him. One day his disciples tried to shoo away a bunch of us who ran up to him. Jesus told them to leave us alone. 'Let them come to me,' he said. He told us that his Father's kingdom belongs to those who have trusting hearts, like children do. Jesus loves kids. I like that about Jesus." (See Mt 19:4; Lk 18:16.)

I Witness

Pentecost

One morning as they were praying together, the whole house began to shake. A strong wind blew through the large room. Suddenly flames appeared above each person's head, like little tongues. The disciples looked at one another in wonder. They no longer felt afraid. Each person was certain about what Jesus had taught. Each one felt eager to share everything he or she had heard from Jesus. They were so energized they immediately went out together and began to tell everyone about Jesus and what he had done for the world.

The people who listened were excited but also confused. They asked one another: "How is it that we each hear these men in our own native language?" (See Acts 2:7–11.) They were amazed! Here they came from different countries with different languages, yet it seemed the disciples spoke all of these languages at once. It was the power of the Holy Spirit at work in the followers of Jesus. Three thousand people were baptized and joined as believers of the Good News that day. It was the day of Pentecost, the day the Church was born.

ONCE UPON A WORD

The word *Pentecost* (PEN-ti-kost) comes from the Greek word for *fifty*. It is a Jewish holiday celebrated fifty days after Passover. In Hebrew it is called *Shavuot*. At Passover Jews remember how God rescued them from slavery in Egypt. They also celebrate the first harvest. On Pentecost, they thank God for giving his Law to Moses on Mount Sinai.

Pentecost is also the name we use for the birthday of the Church. That is because the Holy Spirit came during this Jewish feast. We celebrate Pentecost every year in the Church, fifty days after Easter.

Church of Believers

We see in this story what *church* means. Like the stones or bricks used to build a church, we are members of the Church individually. But the Church is also a community. Stones and bricks *together* form a church building. So, too, all believers together with Jesus form the Church. Church is the calling together of all believers. Jesus himself promised: "I am with you always, to the end of the age" (Mt 28:20). He continues to be with us in the Holy Eucharist. He also promised to send the Holy Spirit. God's Holy Spirit continues to be with the Church to guide her and make her holy. Across the centuries the Church has grown—from the first small group of believers at Pentecost to a large family of faithful women and men all over the world.

SNAPSHOT

Mary, the Mother of Jesus

The Bible tells us that Mary was in the Upper Room on Pentecost. She had been praying with the apostles and disciples after Jesus ascended into heaven. She must have kept their spirits up while they waited for the Holy Spirit. Mary was Jesus' first disciple. She followed him longer than anyone else. And when it came to the Holy Spirit, Mary had lots of experience. The Holy Spirit had made her Jesus' Mother. The Holy Spirit had also revealed to her cousin, Elizabeth, that Mary's child was the Son of God.

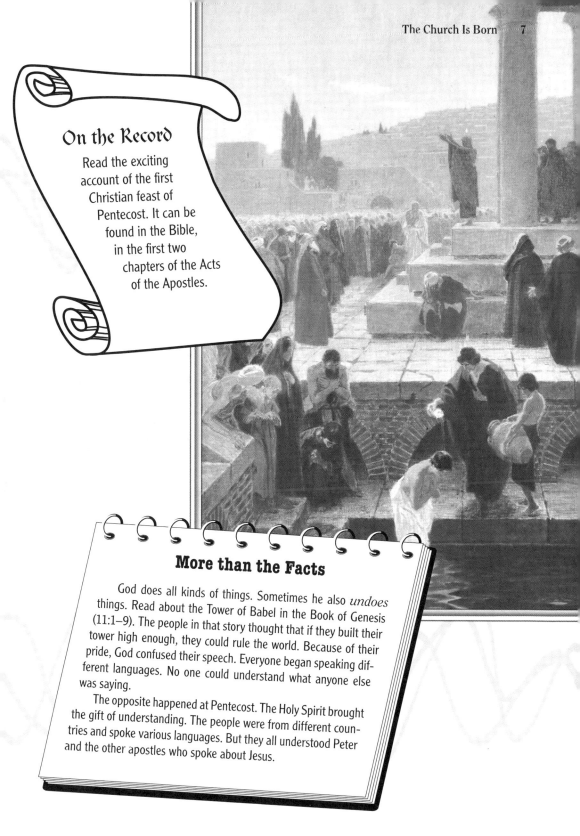

On the Record

Read the exciting
account of the first
Christian feast of
Pentecost. It can be
found in the Bible,
in the first two
chapters of the Acts
of the Apostles.

More than the Facts

God does all kinds of things. Sometimes he also *undoes* things. Read about the Tower of Babel in the Book of Genesis (11:1–9). The people in that story thought that if they built their tower high enough, they could rule the world. Because of their pride, God confused their speech. Everyone began speaking different languages. No one could understand what anyone else was saying.

The opposite happened at Pentecost. The Holy Spirit brought the gift of understanding. The people were from different countries and spoke various languages. But they all understood Peter and the other apostles who spoke about Jesus.

LATEST & GREATEST

One of the most beautiful buildings that existed in the time of Jesus was the Temple. It was in the center of the city because it was the heart of Jewish worship. Today we can go to Jerusalem and visit what's left of that great house of God. Jews and other people gather at the ancient Western Wall. It is also called the Wailing Wall. They stand and pray there to honor God. Many people write their special prayers on slips of paper and place them in the cracks between the stones.

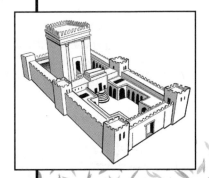

Mystery of History

What is time and how do we keep it, measure it, and record it? What do your yearly school photos tell you about the idea of "time"? Look up some different ways of tracking time: BC/AD, BCE/CE, Roman time, Jewish lunar months and years, Chinese years, the Mayan calendar, and the Ethiopian calendar.

ACTIVITY

Choose a person from one of these New Testament stories: Easter, the Ascension, or Pentecost. Draw a portrait or write a paragraph to give a "snapshot" of this person.

Prayer

Mary, you are called the Queen of the Apostles because you stayed with Jesus' friends in the Upper Room. You prayed with them, consoled them, and encouraged them. As you gave birth to Jesus the Savior, so you witnessed the birth of the Church. Remain with the Church today and always, as our Mother, Teacher, and Queen. Amen.

The Bigger Picture

With the coming of the Holy Spirit, the first followers of Jesus begin to realize what they are being called to do. They are to preach the Good News of salvation to everyone. They are to be brave when future misunderstandings and sufferings come. As we will see, these Jewish believers in Christ will be seen as troublemakers. They will be thrown out of synagogues. They will be separated from family, friends, and the way of life they knew. They will become a new people—the Church.

Chapter 1

AD 30

AD 40

AD 50

AD 60

AD 64—Fire destroys part of Rome.

AD 70

AD 70—Romans destroy the Temple of Jerusalem.

AD 70—Construction begins on the Coliseum (Colosseum) in Rome.

AD 80

AD 79—Mount Vesuvius erupts, burying Pompeii and Herculaneum.

AD 90

Giants of Faith: Peter and Paul

Saint Stephen,
the First Martyr

Saul Becomes Paul

Peter's Vision

Council of Jerusalem

Martyrdom of
Peter and Paul

The first few years after Pentecost were peaceful. Many new people were drawn by Jesus' teachings and by his resurrection. They were also impressed by the kindness of his followers. The young Church began to grow. Those who followed the way of Jesus were mostly faithful Jews who worshiped in the Temple. They also met together to share the words of Jesus and the Eucharist.

Jews who lived in Jerusalem at the time were from different backgrounds. Those who came from the Greek-speaking world were called Hellenists. Those like Jesus, whose native language was Aramaic, were called Nazarenes. Disciples of Jesus came from both of these groups.

Soon conflict arose. The Hellenists claimed that their widows and orphans were being treated like second-class members. According to them, the widows of the Nazarenes were being favored. To restore peace, the apostles appointed seven deacons to care for all the people's needs. Their names were Stephen, Philip, Prochorus, Nicanor, Timon, Parmenes, and Nicholas (Acts 6–9).

SNAPSHOT

Philip the Evangelist

Philip was one of the first seven deacons appointed by the apostles. He left Jerusalem after the death of Stephen. One day God's angel told Philip to go to Gaza. On the way he met an official of the Ethiopian queen. This man was sitting in his chariot, reading from a scroll. Philip saw that the man was puzzled by the writings of the Prophet Isaiah. "Do you understand the prophet's words?" Philip asked. And the man invited Philip into his chariot. Philip then explained that Isaiah was writing about the Savior whom God had promised to send. He told the official how he could find salvation through faith in Jesus Christ. As they came to some water, the official asked Philip to baptize him. After the man was baptized, the Holy Spirit miraculously whisked Philip away to Azotus. There he continued to preach the Good News. (Read the story in Acts 8:26–40.)

On the Record

The first Church history book is part of the Bible. *The Acts of the Apostles* was written by Saint Luke around 64 AD. A Jewish historian, Flavius Josephus (37–100 AD), also wrote about Jesus and the Church in his book, *Antiquities of the Jews*. These books were actually written on scrolls. Josephus said,

"At this time lived a wise man called Jesus. He did amazing deeds and taught truth pleasant to hear. Many Jews followed him and many Greeks as well. And when our important men suggested to Pilate that Jesus be condemned to the cross, he was not abandoned by those who loved him. And those named Christians in his honor are still among us today."

Antiquities of the Jews, book 18, chapter 3, 3

Saint Stephen, the First Martyr

Stephen was a man of great faith and enthusiasm. While he took care of people who needed help, he also spoke publicly about Jesus. Soon Jewish leaders decided he had become too much of a problem. Stephen was arrested. He was accused of insulting God and threatening the Temple. The punishment was death.

Crowds gathered quickly. They piled their coats at the feet of a young man named Saul, then threw rocks at Stephen to kill him. As he lay on the ground, Stephen saw the heavens open and Jesus seated beside God the Father. "Lord Jesus, receive my spirit!" he cried. Moments later he again prayed, "Lord, don't hold this sin against them!" Then he died (Acts 7:1–60). Stephen became the first martyr, the first person to die for his faith in Jesus Christ.

Stephen

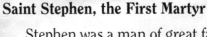

LATEST & GREATEST

Calipers are similar to the protractors we use to measure angles. They were first used around this time. With such instruments, stonemasons and carvers were able to create grand buildings and monuments.

Saul Becomes Paul

The young man who had guarded the coats of those who killed Stephen was Saul of Tarsus. He had permission from the Jewish leaders to arrest Christians who were stirring up trouble. The Jewish leaders wanted to rid Jerusalem of their ideas. Suddenly, everyone seemed to be against the followers of Jesus. Most of the disciples fled Jerusalem, but they did not stop their mission. They continued to teach and baptize people wherever they went. The Church continued to grow.

Saul was determined to put an end to faith in Jesus. One day he set out with other men to round up Christ's disciples in Damascus. On the way there, Saul was suddenly surrounded by a great light. He fell to the ground as a voice called out his name. "Saul, why are you persecuting me?" the voice questioned. Confused, Saul asked, "Who are you?" The voice replied, "I am Jesus, the one you are persecuting. Now get up and go into the city. There you will find out what to do." The light was so bright that it blinded Saul. Completely unable to see, he had to be led into the city by his companions.

Inside Damascus, God had prepared a man named Ananias to heal Saul of his blindness and to baptize him. "I have chosen him to carry my name to nations and kings," Jesus had told Ananias in a vision. (See Acts 9 for all the details.) Saul's experience on the road to Damascus was so powerful that he immediately came to believe in Jesus.

From then on, Saul was known as Paul. He became the greatest missionary the

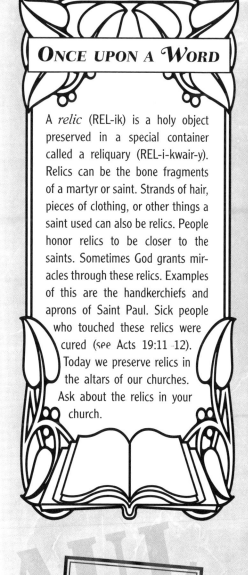

ONCE UPON A WORD

A *relic* (REL-ik) is a holy object preserved in a special container called a reliquary (REL-i-kwair-y). Relics can be the bone fragments of a martyr or saint. Strands of hair, pieces of clothing, or other things a saint used can also be relics. People honor relics to be closer to the saints. Sometimes God grants miracles through these relics. Examples of this are the handkerchiefs and aprons of Saint Paul. Sick people who touched these relics were cured (see Acts 19:11–12). Today we preserve relics in the altars of our churches. Ask about the relics in your church.

Church has ever known. Paul traveled to large cities in Europe and Asia Minor, all the way to Macedonia, Thessalonica, Corinth, and Athens. Sometimes he went alone. Other times he traveled with disciples like Barnabas, Mark, Luke, Titus, or Timothy. Paul had much success in spreading the Gospel, along with a few failures. His missionary journeys were exciting real-life adventures, which even included being shipwrecked!

"Hello! I'm Eutychus and I live in the Greek city of Troas. One evening many people crowded into a big room on the third floor of our house. They came to hear Paul preach about Jesus, called the Christ. I was perched on the windowsill to get a little air. All of my friends and I were there to hear about this new Way of Jesus. I guess I dozed off and fell out the window. Paul, my parents, and others ran down to the street, but I was dead. People tell me that Paul lifted me up and prayed to Christ to restore my life. I only remember opening my eyes to see my mother crying. 'He's alive! He's alive!' she shouted. Now I want to learn everything I can about Jesus Christ." (See Acts 20:7–12.)

I Witness

Peter's Vision

Meanwhile, Peter was also beginning to think of the many people who were not Jews. One day, he saw in a vision a large sheet coming down from heaven. It was filled with all the foods that Jewish people were not allowed to eat. Then he heard a voice telling him to eat some of them. Peter protested that it would be wrong. The voice spoke again, "What God has called clean and good is both clean and good." Around the same time Peter had another vision. This time it was of a man

Mystery of History

In the year 64, a huge fire destroyed a large section of the city of Rome. Was the great fire just an accident? Perhaps. The Emperor Nero, though, blamed it on the Christians. He used this accusation as a reason to put them to death. This was the first organized persecution of Christians in history. Many historians believe that Nero himself may have set the fire. Soon after it, he built a luxurious residence in the neighborhood that had burned down.

asking him to come to his city and bring the message of Jesus to people who were not Jews. Peter realized that Jesus wanted the Church to include everyone. (See Acts 10 for the whole story.)

Council of Jerusalem

The very first Christians were Jewish. But soon more and more non-Jews were attracted to faith in Jesus. This caused confusion and disagreement among church leaders. Some were determined to remain part of the Jewish faith. They wanted all non-Jewish believers in Christ to become Jewish first. Others, like Peter and Paul, recognized that Jesus had died to save everyone. They wanted the Church to be open to people who didn't know or keep the laws of Moses. The matter was finally settled in AD 49 by the Council of Jerusalem. Anyone who sincerely desired to follow Jesus could become a member of the Church.

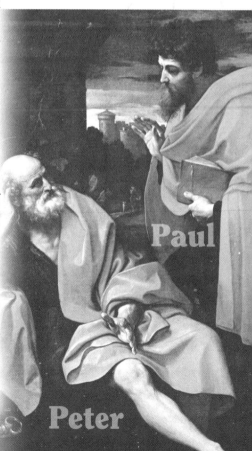

Paul

Peter

Martyrdom of Peter and Paul

Peter and Paul both longed to bring the Good News to Rome. Rome was the center of the civilized world. People from every country came there. The apostles knew that if they preached the Gospel in Rome, visitors of that city would take the message of Jesus back to their own countries. In fact, the Roman Empire had more than 50,000 miles of good roads and many busy ports. That made Rome the perfect starting point for spreading faith in Jesus Christ to the whole world.

Peter secretly made his way to Rome. Paul, however, was brought as a prisoner. The Jewish leaders had been angry with him for teaching about Jesus. They would have killed him earlier, if they had been able. They couldn't because Paul was a Roman citizen. He had the right to appeal to Caesar for judgment. That is exactly what he did.

Around the year AD 64 or 67, the Emperor Nero was persecuting Christians in Rome. Peter and Paul were among the many Christians who died as martyrs. Paul was beheaded, which is how Roman citizens were executed at the time. Peter, on the other hand, was crucified. It is said that Peter did not consider himself worthy to die the way Jesus had. So he asked to be hung on the cross upside down. The relics of Peter and Paul have always been venerated by Christians in Rome. These two apostles are considered the pillars that have supported the Church throughout its history.

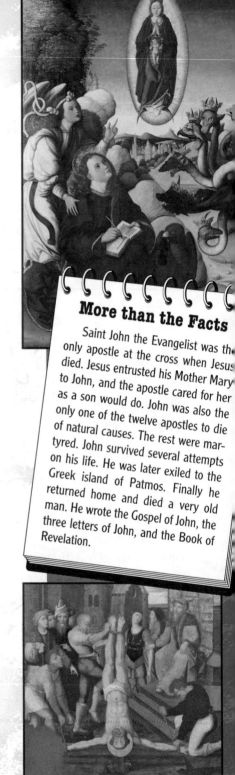

More than the Facts

Saint John the Evangelist was the only apostle at the cross when Jesus died. Jesus entrusted his Mother Mary to John, and the apostle cared for her as a son would do. John was also the only one of the twelve apostles to die of natural causes. The rest were martyred. John survived several attempts on his life. He was later exiled to the Greek island of Patmos. Finally he returned home and died a very old man. He wrote the Gospel of John, the three letters of John, and the Book of Revelation.

ACTIVITY

The Bible is holy. It is even more worthy of veneration than the relics of the saints. The Bible is God's word and his message of salvation. Talk to your family, teachers, or classmates about preparing a special place to display the Bible. How will you decorate this place? When we spend time reflecting on the Scriptures, our minds and hearts become "reliquaries" for God's word! Read a short piece of the Bible every day. Be sure to think about what it says—and then live by it.

Prayer

Lord, this first century of the Church was a time of giants. The first Christians were so enthusiastic about your life and teachings. These men and women lived faith-filled lives and shared the Good News with everyone. Give the joy and excitement of discipleship to me as well.
Amen.

The Bigger Picture

The very first Christians heard Jesus preach and saw him work miracles. Jesus himself taught them how to live. As time went on, however, these eyewitnesses began to die. It became clear that to continue passing on faith in Christ, his followers would need instruction. They would need a written account of what Jesus said and did.

As time passed, some of the apostles began to write letters about Jesus. The letters were read aloud in Christian communities. Early disciples also wrote books of history (the Acts of the Apostles) and prophecy (the Book of Revelation). Their words gave Christians hope and helped them grow in holiness. Jesus' life and teachings were written down in the Gospels by four "evangelists"—Matthew, Mark, Luke, and John. Much, but not all, of what was written about Christian faith was collected. It became known as the New Testament.

The first century witnessed a great geographical spread of the Christian faith. Since at that time a message could only be spread by word of mouth or by letter, the apostles began to make missionary adventures. Saint Paul made several amazing journeys to start churches. He followed up his visits by writing letters to the Christians of those churches. In addition to Paul, Saint Thomas made his way east to India, where he preached the Gospel. A vibrant Catholic Christian Church exists there to this day. Saint James the Greater was another great missionary apostle. He brought the faith west to Spain. In just a few years, the Church spread from Jerusalem and Rome to the ends of the known world.

Chapter 2

2nd century—Buddhism is brought from India to China.

53–117—During his lifetime, the Roman Emperor Trajan extends the Roman Empire to include Mesopotamia and Assyria.

AD 105

105—A form of paper is invented in China by Ts'ai Lun by grinding and soaking plant fiber.

AD 115

around 117—Parthians (in what is Iran today) develop full suits of armor for soldiers and horses.

AD 125

124—The Pantheon (a temple dedicated to all the Roman gods) in Rome is completed.

AD 135

135—The final diaspora, or spreading out, of the Jews occurs. Forced to leave their homelands, Jews spread throughout Europe, Africa, and the Middle East.

AD 145

27 BC to AD 180—This time is known as the *Pax Romana*: a time of peace in the Roman Empire.

AD 155

AD 165

Lots of Trouble

Catholics often refer to the Church as our Mother. This is because we receive the life of Christ as grace through the Church. We are the children of God, but also sons and daughters of the Church. Like a good mother, the Church teaches us, nurtures us with the sacraments, and guides us through this life to heaven.

Much growth took place in the second century of the Church's life. The Church reached out to many other peoples and cultures. When we look at the great number of people who make up the Church all around the world today, it is easy to forget how small the Church was at the beginning. It may also be hard to imagine the enormous dangers our Church faced from the start.

Map of the Flavian Amphitheater

2nd century

"Hi, my name is Lucius. I've been watching the workers build the gigantic new arena near my house. People say it will hold at least 50,000 people. Everyone is calling it the Colosseum, but its official name is the Flavian Amphitheater. Our emperor, Vespasian, belongs to the Flavian family. He said he is building the arena as a gift to the people of Rome. There will be animal hunts, horse races, and gladiator contests. The arena can even be filled with water to stage battles between ships! Everything sounds so exciting. But I don't think I'll want to see gladiators fighting to the death. What a waste of life!"

I Witness

Crime to Believe

The Roman Empire was large and included people from many cultures. These people practiced a variety of pagan religions. Because their religions had numerous gods, they were similar to that of Rome. The people from the pagan religions simply added the Roman gods—and the Emperor—to their own gods.

The Christian and Jewish faiths, however, were different. Christians and Jews believe in only one true God. That was contrary to the official religion of Rome. Many faithful Christians refused to participate in pagan rituals. They also refused to honor the emperor as a god. Because of this, they were viewed as traitors.

The Emperor Trajan saw the Christians as a threat to the empire. He decided to make their religion illegal. During his reign, in AD 112, it became a crime to believe in Jesus. Nevertheless, the Church continued to grow in numbers and in strength.

the Emperor Trajan

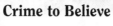

LATEST & GREATEST

Between the years 18 and 125, an important pagan temple in Rome was rebuilt. The Pantheon was entirely redesigned, with a round interior topped by a dome. At the base, the walls are twenty feet thick; however, the dome is only seven or eight feet thick and has a large opening at the top. The material for the dome is what made this structure possible. Its mixture of sand, volcanic ash, gravel, and quicklime is much lighter in weight than the massive brick and concrete walls. The Pantheon remains standing today, and has been turned into a Catholic church.

More than the Facts

The Chinese have been exporting things for thousands of years. In the second century AD, many of the products popular throughout the Roman Empire were made in China. Romans loved the woven silk, lacquered wood, porcelain goods, and paper they imported from the Far East.

ONCE UPON A WORD

Heresy (HAIR-uh-see) is the denial, distortion, or rejection of a truth of God taught by the Church. Sometimes heresy is a misunderstanding of the faith. Other times it over-emphasizes one truth at the expense of another. If someone willfully holds on to a heresy, that person can end up being cut off from the Church.

Councils

The Church was still growing in its understanding of faith in Jesus. Along the way, many different views spread. These teachings often conflicted with each other. In order to stay unified, the pope and the bishops met together in councils. They prayed over these new ideas and discussed them. Church leaders knew it was their responsibility to define what was true and what wasn't. They also decided how best to present the truths they were teaching. (See downloadable index for a chart of the Church councils). They wanted to be clear about what everyone should believe.

Heresies

Some people who tried to teach about God and his Church made mistakes. Several of the things they taught sounded good, but ended up being incorrect or false. These false teachings are called *heresies*. (See downloadable index for a chart of the major heresies.)

Many of these teachers were humble enough to admit they were wrong and change what they were teaching. Unfortunately, however, some of them refused to accept the authority of the Church. They were convinced that they were right and the Church was wrong. They would not change what they were teaching. These heretics caused a lot of trouble, division, and confusion for the Church.

Heretics always think they have a "better" idea about Christian faith than the Church does. One of these men was Marcion (144). He spread many false teachings about

Mystery of History

In the second century AD, an Egyptian astronomer and mathematician named Ptolemy wrote a book about the universe. Ptolemy believed that the earth was at the center of a larger sphere. He held that the sun, moon, and stars all traveled around the earth. People thought Ptolemy was right. It took fifteen more centuries before anyone successfully challenged his theory. Do you know who taught that the sun was the center of the universe? What do we know about the sun today?

On the Record

Saint Irenaeus gives an example of how someone became a bishop. Here he is speaking of Saint Polycarp (69–155): "Not only was he taught by the apostles and lived in friendship with those who had seen Christ. He also received his appointment from the apostles as bishop in the Church of Smyrna in Asia"

(*Against Heresies*, III, 3).

the Ptolemaic system

Christianity. He taught that Jesus was not the Son of God, but just a messenger of God.

Heresies don't only have to do with what we believe. Sometimes a heresy has to do with *how* we live what we believe. A group known as Donatists, for example, said that Christians did not have high enough standards or do enough penance. Other heresies said that Christian teaching was too strict. Gnostics (NAWS–ticks) believed that if we love, we don't need to worry about obeying rules—not even God's laws.

Marcion

SNAPSHOT

Saint Ignatius of Antioch (35–107)

We know little about Ignatius' life except that he was bishop of the Church in Antioch (a city now in Turkey). During the reign of Emperor Trajan, Ignatius was arrested and brought to Rome for trial. Along the way, he wrote seven letters to various Christian communities. In his letters Ignatius instructed and encouraged the Christians in their faith. He also wrote to the Christians of Rome, asking them not to prevent his martyrdom. In his writings the term "Catholic Church" is used for the first time. Ignatius was eventually condemned and sentenced to execution. He was devoured by lions in the Colosseum. Today many theologians use Ignatius' letters to teach what the earliest Christians believed about the Eucharist and to defend the Catholic faith.

Early Church Fathers

Numerous bishops and teachers at this time wrote books and letters to explain Church beliefs. Someone even wrote an instructional story called *The Shepherd of Hermas*. Many of them were executed for their faith in Christ.

Saint Polycarp of Smyrna

Polycarp (69–155) was a bishop. He wrote letters of instruction to various communities. After returning from a trip to Rome, he was arrested and put to death for being a Christian. Polycarp was a highly respected Church leader. He had been a disciple of Saint John the Apostle. Because he was very old when he was killed, Polycarp's death shocked the Christians of his day.

Polycarp

Saint Justin Martyr

The Church continued to develop her understanding of God and his mysteries. This was due to the work of many educated persons. One of these was a lay philosopher named Justin (100–165). At the time most people believed in many gods. Justin had been born into a pagan family and received the best education. When he became a Christian, he used all his knowledge and skill to convince others that Christianity was the truth. Justin was an *apologist*. An apologist does not apologize for believing in Christ, but defends the Christian faith. Justin was effective because he could explain how the Church's teachings made sense. We can still read his work today. The greatest defense Justin made, though, was holding on to what he believed no matter the cost. Because Justin refused to worship the emperor as a god, he was put to death.

Saint Irenaeus

Irenaeus (around 130–200) was the bishop of Lyons in France. He wrote a famous book called *Against Heresies*. In it, Irenaeus explained how the heretics were wrong. He also reminded his readers of the basic teachings of the true Catholic faith.

TRINUS
UNITAS

Tertullian

Tertullian

Around the same time, a teacher named Tertullian (200) lived in the city of Carthage in North Africa. He was making a big impact on the Church of his day. Tertullian invented new words to explain mysteries that are hard to understand. All the great Church teachers looked to Tertullian for help in teaching the faith. They used his terms and concepts to explain the teachings of Christianity. They used his work to judge whether or not new ideas were correct.

Tertullian coined words like *Trinity* and *sacrament*. As Christians, we believe in one God who is three divine Persons. Tertullian took the adjective *three* (in Latin, *trinus*) and the word for *unity* (*unitas*) and put them together. *Trinitas* means a perfect unity of three. We say *the* Trinity because there is no other trinity except God: Father, Son, and Holy Spirit. Tertullian also put together the Latin words *sacra-* (which means "holy"*)*, and *-ment* (which means "an action"). A sacrament is an action that makes something holy come about.

SACRA
MENT

ACTIVITY

Look up information about how the Romans reenacted great sea battles in the Colosseum. Then see if you can stage a naval battle. Fill a bathtub or large bucket with water, and use paper boats.

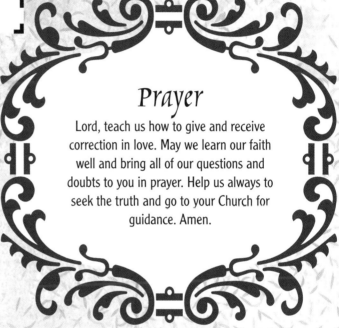

Prayer

Lord, teach us how to give and receive correction in love. May we learn our faith well and bring all of our questions and doubts to you in prayer. Help us always to seek the truth and go to your Church for guidance. Amen.

The Bigger Picture

The second century was a time for development of Church teaching. It was a time in which errors had to be corrected. Nonetheless, the Church was still in its infancy. This same growth and correction will continue throughout the Church's history. Heresies still appear today, and people still misinterpret and misrepresent the faith. The Church continues to call the bishops together in councils to clarify her message.

The martyrdoms of early Christians were just a hint at the greater waves of persecution that would follow. We will see this in the next chapter. Even today the challenges to Christian faith can involve great danger and large-scale persecution.

Chapter 3

AD 200

201—Empress Jinjū rules in Japan after her husband's death until her son accedes to the throne in 269.

AD 212

AD 224

AD 236

AD 248

AD 260

265–317—China is reunited from three kingdoms to one as the Western Jin Dynasty.

268—Goths invade and sack Athens, Corinth, and Sparta.

AD 272

271—An early form of compass is used by the Chinese.

AD 284

284—Diocletian becomes emperor of Rome.

AD 296

300—North Africa is mostly Christian.

Martyrs and Missionaries

The numbers of new Christians grew rapidly everywhere. Missionaries followed the example of Saints Peter and Paul and the other apostles. These men and women were enthusiastic about the teachings of Christ. They traveled to faraway places where people did not know about Jesus. Wherever they went, the missionaries spoke about what Jesus Christ had done for them. They invited others to believe in him as well. One missionary, Saint Denis, was sent by the Church to Gaul (later known as France). He became the first bishop of Paris. Denis successfully converted many to faith in Christ. He was martyred there in the year 250.

Persecution in the Roman Empire

The persecution of Christians continued in waves throughout this century. Not everything was going well in the vast Roman Empire. Discontent among some of the subjects of Rome caused trade to decline. Many Romans were nervous about their future.

In such uncertain times, the people appealed to their false gods for help. Some said that things were not right because the gods were angry that the Christians refused to honor them. Christians had to be more careful than ever. They could never feel completely free to practice their beliefs. Besides, Trajan's law still existed. Christianity was a crime, and any Roman leader could use the law to put Christians to death.

"Hello, my name is Sylvester. I am a Christian, but please don't tell anyone. The pagans don't understand our religion. They are throwing every Christian they discover into jail. Most of the prisoners will be killed. I have a friend, Tarcisius, who volunteered to carry the Eucharist to them. He plans to hide the Body of Christ by wrapping it up in a cloth under his tunic. He's only twelve, but he is brave enough to help console his friends before their martyrdom. I am afraid for him, because I know that if he's caught, he might end up becoming a martyr, too."

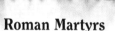

Roman Martyrs

Many Christians held onto their faith in Jesus Christ and his Church despite the threat of suffering and death. They had experienced the saving love of Jesus and were willing to sacrifice everything for him. Popes, bishops, priests, deacons, and laymen and laywomen were martyred. The people of Rome were impressed by their willingness to die for their faith. Christians exhibited courage and even joy in the face of suffering. These qualities inspired many to question their beliefs and think seriously about Christianity.

Mystery of History

Historians believe that about 300,000 people died for the faith in the first century. By the twentieth century, millions were martyred. And today, millions of Christians around the world are still being persecuted. Why do you think so many people were and are willing to risk—or even lose—their lives to follow Jesus?

Rich Martyrs

People from every social class had become Christian. No one was safe from the persecutions, not even the wealthy. Saint Cecilia, a young noblewoman of Rome, is an example. Her parents arranged a marriage for her to a young man named Valerian. On the night of their wedding, Cecilia told him that she belonged totally to Christ. Valerian listened to her explanation of Christianity and became a Christian himself. Together they suffered martyrdom.

tradition holds that even in death Cecilia professed her faith in the Trinity—3 in 1

More than the Facts

ICHTHYS is an acronym made from the letters of the Greek words I*esous* CH*ristos* TH*eou Yios Soter*, that is, *Jesus Christ, God's Son, Savior.* It was a declaration of faith in Jesus. The word *ichthys* itself means fish. It became a secret symbol, used by Christians to identify one another and to mark places of worship.

Fish drawings are found on the walls within the Catacombs of Priscilla (in use from the second to the fourth centuries); this is one of the many catacombs located near Rome. Catacombs are underground cemeteries. They contain passageways lined with shelves where people were buried. Larger rooms at the end of these passageways were used as churches. Christian communities would gather in secret to celebrate the Eucharist. The Catacombs of Priscilla also feature one of the earliest known paintings of Mary and an icon of the Good Shepherd.

SANCTA PERPETVA • SANCTA FELICITAS

On the Record

"Remain strong in the faith and love one another. Do not be afraid because of what has happened to us." This is what Saint Perpetua said to other imprisoned African Christians waiting to die for Christ. Perpetua was a young noblewoman who left behind her husband and young son. Her companion, Saint Felicity, was a slave. Felicity had just given birth to a child in prison. The two women were martyred with many others in Carthage on March 7, 203. *The Passion of Saint Perpetua, Saint Felicitas, and Their Companions* is an authentic account of their imprisonment. It was written in part by Saint Perpetua herself.

Military Martyrs

The Roman Empire had the most powerful army in the world. It was particularly shocking, then, when loyal Roman soldiers were executed as traitors. Saint Maurice (Mauritius in Latin) was the commander of the Roman legion from the city of Thebes in Egypt. In the year 287, the emperor called for the 6,600 soldiers of the Theban legion to put down a revolt of Germanic tribes. Maurice and his men, however, were Christians. They refused the emperor's order to attack the Christians of the area. Threatened with death, the soldiers remained faithful to Christ. As a result, the entire Theban legion was martyred by their fellow Roman soldiers at Agaunum. The place is now known as the Valley of Saint Maurice in Switzerland. Saint Maurice was later named the patron saint of the Holy Roman Emperors.

Saint Antony of Egypt

At eighteen, Saint Antony of Egypt (251–356) gave away all he owned and began a life of prayer and penance. When he was thirty he went to live alone in the desert. Antony had a reputation for holiness and wisdom. Many, including the Emperor Constantine, sought him for spiritual advice. In time, Antony inspired others to imitate his monastic way of life. Monks separate themselves from the world and dedicate their lives completely to prayer and spiritual works.

Antony made at least two trips to Alexandria, a great city in Egypt. His first journey was to encourage those being persecuted for their faith. Later, he returned to help fight the influence of Arius, a heretical priest. When it was time to go back home, Antony retired to a mountain cave. Eventually he organized those who had settled nearby. He gathered them into a community of hermits and gave them a rule of life. Today Saint Antony is known as the founder of Christian monasticism.

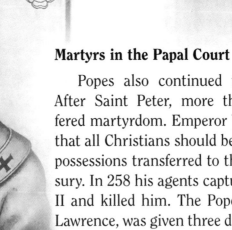

XISTVS ·II·PP·GRÆCVS

Martyrs in the Papal Court

Popes also continued to be executed. After Saint Peter, more than twenty suffered martyrdom. Emperor Valerian decreed that all Christians should be killed and their possessions transferred to the imperial treasury. In 258 his agents captured Pope Sixtus II and killed him. The Pope's chief deacon, Lawrence, was given three days to collect the Church's riches and turn them over to the authorities. Lawrence quickly distributed

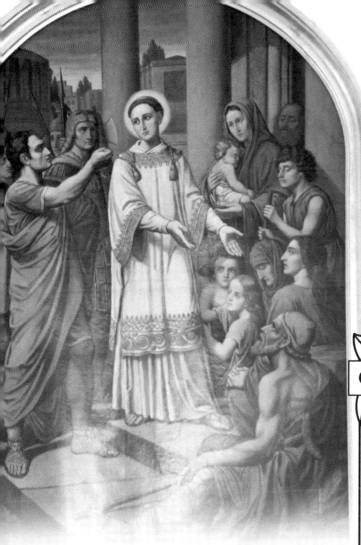

ONCE UPON A WORD

Ecclesiastical (eh-klee-zee-AS-ti-kuhl) is an adjective that means "of the Church." The Church adopted this word from the Greek word *ekklesia*, which means "an assembly." When we come together as Church, it is a holy assembly. We also speak of ecclesiastical history, ecclesiastical ministry, and ecclesiology. Priests are sometimes called ecclesiastics.

everything he could to the poor of Rome. When he appeared in court, he brought with him people who were poor, crippled, and blind. Lawrence presented *them* as the Church's treasure. He was immediately condemned to a slow and painful death. He was tied to a large iron grill that had been placed over fiery coals. According to legend, Saint Lawrence's last words to his executioners were, "Turn me over. I'm done on this side."

LATEST & GREATEST

The wheelbarrow was first invented in China. Imagine what a useful invention it was for farmers and merchants. It was like having an extra-large basket with a handle and one or two wheels. People could push their crops or goods to market without a horse or mule.

Mistaken Teachers

The Church of the third century also had great teachers. Origen (185–254) was one of them. He was a famous preacher in Alexandria, Egypt, before he was even ordained a priest. Origen wrote many persuasive books, including one on martyrdom and another on prayer. He ran into trouble, however. Some of the ideas Origen taught were heretical. Although he was careful to distinguish his own opinions from Church teaching, bishops forbid Christians from reading his books. They did this to protect the unity and truths of the faith.

Like Origen, Tertullian (around 150–225) was a pioneer in Christian theology. Tertullian once said that the blood of martyrs is like a seed of faith enlarging the Church with new believers. But like Origen, Tertullian wrote things about the faith that contained errors. Nonetheless, these two theologians contributed greatly to the Church's understanding of Christian belief.

ACTIVITY

Look for a book in the library or for information online about the Roman catacombs. How many catacombs were beneath the city of Rome? How did the Christians keep their gatherings hidden from Roman officials?

Prayer

Lord Jesus, I am proud to be a Christian. Thank you for the witness of so many martyrs and missionaries. Give strength and perseverance to Christians who suffer today because they believe in you. Help all missionaries and teachers of the faith. Make them united, creative, and joyful witnesses to your Gospel message. Amen.

The Bigger Picture

For centuries the Roman Empire was the greatest power in the world. By the third century, however, Rome was experiencing problems. The tribal nations to the north were restless, and the peoples to the east were gaining strength. Natural disasters such as droughts and plagues occurred. These, along with political intrigue and a weak economy, caused a crisis within the empire. The situation reflected badly on the emperors. Many individuals and groups spent their energy trying to make the empire strong again. The result was a succession of corrupt and weak emperors. Rome was suffering; the great empire was beginning its long decline.

Throughout history ever since, people and societies hungry for power have tried to recreate the glory Rome once had. Examples can be found in the rise of Constantinople, the Holy Roman emperors, Moscow and the Russian czar, Napoleon, Germany's kaiser, and even Hitler and the Nazi conquest of Europe. In fact, the German word *kaiser* and the Russian word *czar* both come from the word *Caesar*.

Chapter 4

300–350—Teotihuacán (an ancient Mesoamerican city) extends its control of Mayan cities (present-day Guatemala).

301—The baptism of Armenian King Tiridates III makes Armenia the first Christian nation.

314—The *Schola cantorum* (choir school) is founded at Rome by Pope Sylvester I.

AD 312

AD 324

326—Ground is broken for the first St. Peter's Basilica.

330—Constantine establishes the city of Constantinople, formerly Byzantium (and present-day Istanbul), as capital of the Roman Empire.

AD 336

AD 348

AD 360

AD 372

AD 384

391—Pagan rituals are outlawed in the Roman Empire, so most people become Christian.

AD 396

Rule of Constantine

41

Waves of persecution had swept over the followers of Christ since the beginning of the Church. The persecution begun by Emperor Diocletian in 303, however, was the worst of them all. The Roman Empire was crumbling. In some regions, it was not even strong enough to defend itself. Diocletian was convinced that Christians were the cause of these problems. He felt they had angered the Roman gods. So Diocletian ordered that churches and holy books be burned. He demanded the imprisonment of every Christian. Many were condemned to death.

4th century

Saint Sebastian

Even people loyal to Rome were caught up in this new persecution. Sebastian was one of these. A good and capable soldier, Sebastian was also a Christian. He had served proudly in the army of Rome and was personally known to the emperor. Sebastian's first loyalty, however, was to Christ and his Church. When it became necessary to choose between his military career and his faith, Sebastian did not hesitate. He encouraged other imprisoned Christians. Because of this, Sebastian was accused of treason. Diocletian ordered that he be executed by archers. After this took place, he was left for dead.

Mystery of History

One of the most famous travelers of the fourth century was a woman named Egeria. Quite a bit of mystery surrounds her life. We don't know a lot about her. We know that she spent three years visiting places in the Holy Land associated with Jesus. It seems she kept a detailed diary of her trip, but much of it has been lost. Egeria made notes about the people she met, the liturgies she encountered, and the adventures she had. Many have speculated about her identity. Was she a member of a royal group touring the Holy Land? Was she a nun making a religious pilgrimage? Where did her trip begin? Did she ever go on another such trip, as it seems she had planned?

Sebastian being tended by Irene and her maid

A good Christian widow, who was present, realized that Sebastian was still alive. She brought him to her house and nursed him back to health. After he recovered, the woman expected Sebastian to flee Rome. But Sebastian was very courageous. He went right back to helping Christians in prison. When Diocletian found out, he had Sebastian beaten to death.

Diocletian

Changes in the Roman Empire

Emperor Diocletian realized how difficult it was for one man to control the vast Roman Empire. Distances were too great and the army too large and widespread. Enemy attacks were also becoming too frequent. So Diocletian divided the empire into two parts. He became ruler of the Eastern Empire and appointed Maximian ruler of the West. Diocletian settled in Byzantium, in present-day Turkey. Maximian set up his capital in Rome. Each emperor was give the title "Augustus." Each had an assistant emperor with the title "Caesar." To ensure some stability in leadership, the Caesars were supposed to take over as the next Augustuses. This system led to problems, however, including rivalry for power.

Things began to happen for the Church as well. For three hundred years it had been dangerous to be a Christian. In 312, however, a new emperor of the West changed that. Constantine, the emperor of the West, went out to battle Maxentius, the emperor of the East. Both rulers wanted to be sole master of Rome. What occurred in this confrontation would change the lives of Christians from then on.

Maximian

LATEST & GREATEST

Emperor Constantine established the seven-day week in 321. Previously, Rome had used both a seven-day week and an eight-day week. Constantine wanted everyone to follow the week spoken of in the Bible. He made Sunday the first day of the week in honor of Christ's resurrection.

Maxentius

Constantine

Emperor Constantine

Constantine was not a baptized Christian. His mother Helen, however, was. As Constantine prepared for battle, he prayed to the Christian God for success. Enemy troops were approaching the Milvian Bridge, which crossed the Tiber River not far from Rome. When Constantine reached the bridge, he saw a vision in the sky. A large Chi–Rho (formed from the Greek letters that look like "X" and "P"), a symbol of Christianity, appeared. With it were the words *in hoc signe vinces*, which mean "in this sign you will triumph." Seeing this miraculous sign, Constantine and his army gained the courage they needed. Constantine placed the symbol on his banners and on the shields of his soldiers. His army was victorious.

The Edict of Milan

Constantine's victory was also a victory for Christianity. The next year, he, as emperor of the West, and Licinius, the next emperor of the East, issued a joint statement called the Edict of Milan. It granted Christians freedom to worship publicly. All the property that had been taken away from Christians was returned to them. In fact, Constantine gave his own palace on Lateran Hill to the Church. It later became the site of the Lateran Basilica, the pope's cathedral in Rome. Constantine gave his mother, Saint Helen, access to the empire's treasury. She built churches and cared for the poor. It is said that Helen searched for and found the true cross on which Jesus died. During this time the sacraments were celebrated, instruction in the faith was given openly, and many people were baptized—including Constantine himself. The Church was free to grow again.

On the Record

In 313 the emperors of the West and the East issued the Edict of Milan. This edict granted religious freedom to everyone. Here is how the edict begins:

"When I, Constantine Augustus, and I, Licinius Augustus, met near Milan, we considered aspects of public welfare and security. Among other things we looked at the laws dealing with the worship of God. We grant to Christians and all others the right to follow the religion they prefer. We have decided that no one should be denied the opportunity to wholeheartedly observe the Christian religion. Anyone who wishes to may now observe the Christian religion freely, openly, and without disturbance."

Important Saints of the 4th Century

This was a century of great and saintly teachers of the faith; there are almost too many to count! In the East were Saint Athanasius (296–373); Saint Nicholas of Myra (270–343), known to us as Santa Claus; Saint Cyril of Jerusalem (315–386); Saint Gregory Nazianzen (329–390); Saint Basil the Great (329–379), as well as his sister Saint Macrina (327–379) and his brother Saint Gregory of Nyssa (330–395); and the preacher Saint John Chrysostom (347–407). In the West were Saint Hilary of Poitiers (around 315–368); the former Roman soldier, Saint Martin of Tours (336–397); and Saint Ambrose (339–397). Each of these holy people contributed to how the Church understood and lived faith in Jesus Christ.

It was a time of innovation. Saint Ambrose, the archbishop of Milan, introduced rhyming hymns to Christian worship. Saint Eusebius (around 263–340), bishop of Caesarea in Palestine, is called "the father of Church history." His book *Ecclesiastical History* made note of the traditional places where the apostles were sent.

"I just heard something amazing! My friend Elena told me that last night someone threw a sack of gold coins into her house. Elena's oldest sister wanted to get married, but the family had no money for her dowry. Now they do—and enough for all three girls, too. People told them that without enough money they might have to become slaves. Well, you can imagine how happy they are today. Elena's father thinks the money came from Bishop Nicholas, the bishop of our city of Myra. In fact, her father has gone now to town to thank him. Oh, my name is Dora, and I just can't stop dancing for joy!"

I Witness

Arius

The Council of Nicea

The single most important event in the Church at this time happened at the Council of Nicea in 325. A priest named Arius (250–336) had been confusing people. He taught that Jesus was a special man but not God. Arius agreed that Jesus had been sent by God. But according to Arius, Jesus had been created like other human beings; he was not equal to God.

Bishop Alexander of Alexandria, Egypt, along with Emperor Constantine, called all the bishops of the Church together. They listened carefully, both to Arius' reasoning and Saint Athanasius' response. Then the council of bishops decided that Arius was wrong. They instructed him to stop his heretical teaching. They also wrote a statement of true teaching. This statement of faith is called the Nicene Creed. We still use it today. The Council of Nicea also decided how to figure the date for the Easter celebration.

ONCE UPON A WORD

Today, with cell phones and computers, we communicate a lot. We know that speaking to another person face-to-face is also communicating. When we communicate, we share our thoughts, beliefs, and affection. When someone is *excommunicated* (eks-kuh-MYOO-ni-kayt-ed) it means that communication between that person and the Church has been cut off. A person who teaches heresies against the faith of Christ is officially cut off from everything we share as God's People: sacraments, grace, and community.

The First Council of Constantinople

Later, in 381, Pope Damasus and Emperor Theodosius called the first Council of Constantinople. They wanted to clarify what the Council of Nicea had taught. This time the Church condemned a heresy known as Modalism or Sabellianism. The heresy was taught by a priest named Sabellius. He denied that there were really three Persons in the Trinity. The Modalists taught that God was only one Person who presented himself in three different ways. To counteract this heresy, the council Fathers added the section on the Holy Spirit to the Nicene Creed.

More than the Facts

At the Council of Rome in 382 the bishops decided to collect and organize all the books we know today as the Bible. There were many writings to choose from. Not all of them made it onto the final list. The bishops had to judge which books were inspired by God and which were just good accounts of salvation history. The final collection is called the Canon, or officially accepted books, of the Bible. In all there are forty-six books in the Old Testament and twenty-seven books in the New Testament. A few years after the Canon was organized, Saint Jerome began translating the Bible. It had originally been written in Hebrew and Greek. Jerome translated the Bible into Latin, the language of the Roman Empire. He completed his translation, known as the Vulgate, in 405.

A Christian Empire

In the same year, 381, Emperor Theodosius declared Christianity to be the official religion of the Roman Empire. Many still practiced paganism, Judaism, and other religions. But more and more inhabitants embraced faith in Jesus.

SNAPSHOT

Saint Monica

Saint Monica (332–387) lived in a city called Hippo. It was a seaport city in northern Africa, in what is now Algeria. Monica's husband, Patricius, was not a Christian like her. Still, he allowed Monica to raise their two sons in the faith.

At that time infants did not receive baptism. Children were instructed in Church teaching, but they usually waited until they were adults to be baptized. Monica's son Augustine (354–430), however, never asked for baptism. He studied ancient philosophy and became a teacher and speaker. Despite his talents, he picked up many sinful habits over the years. His mother Monica cried many tears over him. She prayed daily for his conversion.

Some time later, Augustine took a job teaching public speaking in Milan. While there, he happened to hear the bishop preach. This bishop was the great Saint Ambrose. At first, Augustine was impressed by the bishop's excellent preaching skill. Eventually, he realized that what the bishop preached, and what his mother had always said about Jesus Christ, was true. He turned away from sin and asked to be baptized. Augustine later acknowledged that his mother's prayers and good example were what helped him the most. He went on to become a priest and bishop of Hippo. His brilliant mind made him one of the greatest theologians in Christian history.

ACTIVITY

Look up more information on popular pilgrimage destinations. Where would you travel if you wanted to grow in faith? Make a map. Who—and what—would you take with you? What would you leave behind? Make a list.

Prayer

Thank you, God, for all the good things that happened in the fourth century. We are grateful especially for the Nicene Creed, which we recite during Mass on Sundays and special holy days. When we pray together what we believe, you, Lord, make the Church united and stronger. Help us to become more of a family of faith. Amen.

The Bigger Picture

The fourth century was a transforming time for the Church. Now that Christianity was legalized, Church leaders had greater freedom to act. They could more easily resolve disagreements and misunderstandings about the faith. Councils of bishops were able to define and clarify what Christians believe. They also identified errors in belief. Ideas that opposed official teaching could be corrected. All of this made it easier for Christians to be united in faith. Nonetheless, some heresies were difficult to stamp out. Arianism, for example, lasted hundreds of years after the death of Arius.

The fourth century also saw the beginning of a more universal idea of holiness. Since people were able to follow Christ openly, it was easier to observe holiness in those around them. In past times, only the apostles and martyrs were recognized as saints. From now on, many more examples of holiness came to light. Christians of every walk of life gave witness to their faith.

Monasteries, too, began to thrive as centers of faith and learning in every corner of the Christian world. These monasteries built up the Church. They would prove to be a great means in preserving not only faith but culture and civilization as well in the difficult centuries ahead.

Chapter 5

AD 410

401—Pope Innocent I establishes the Petrine Doctrine by claiming universal authority over the Roman Catholic Church.

410—Alaric, King of the Goths, sacks Rome.

AD 420

AD 430

432—Saint Patrick arrives in Ireland and begins to convert the Irish.

AD 440

AD 450

452—Pope Leo the Great (d. 461) meets Attila the Hun.

455—Vandals conquer Rome.

AD 460

AD 470

476—Romulus Augustus, the last Roman emperor of the West (475), is deposed by the Goths.

AD 480

AD 490

500—Tea from India is brought to China.

Days of Danger

The fifth century began as a time of peace and security for the Church. Christians were free to live and worship openly. The example of how they lived influenced others to become Christians. Whole cities and nations discovered and embraced the Gospel of Jesus.

For people living beyond the Roman Empire, however, life was becoming more difficult. The spread of heresies, the outbreak of wars, and the migration of large numbers of people brought much uncertainty to daily life. In fact, whole tribes were on the move again. They had come down from the north and settled just beyond the Danube and Rhine Rivers long years before. Where would they go now?

Invaders

Barbarians, as they were known to the Romans, were groups of warriors used to constant raiding and fighting. The very sight of these long-haired men dressed in shabby clothes, draped in animal skins, and wielding crude axes and spears terrified the more civilized populations of the Roman world. The army on the borders of the empire struggled to keep them out. Ultimately, however, Rome failed. In 410 the Goths, a fierce group of Germanic tribes led by Alaric, attacked Rome in search of food.

Eventually the Goths were subdued. Some were allowed to settle within Roman borders. Though the Goths were not well disciplined, the Romans came to admire their strength and courage. Soon Rome even enlisted their help to fight off other invaders.

5th c

Alaric

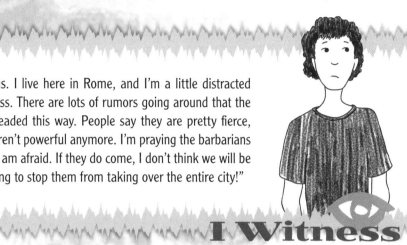

The arrangement benefited both groups for a short time. Then Rome took advantage of them. They sent the Goths into the fiercest battles. Their children were taken away as slaves, and their crops were heavily taxed.

"Hello! I'm Darius. I live here in Rome, and I'm a little distracted or nervous, I guess. There are lots of rumors going around that the barbarians are headed this way. People say they are pretty fierce, and our armies aren't powerful anymore. I'm praying the barbarians don't come, but I am afraid. If they do come, I don't think we will be able to do anything to stop them from taking over the entire city!"

I Witness

Attila the Hun

The Roman Empire lived with constant fear of attack by barbarian tribes. In 402 it was forced to move its capital to Ravenna, 175 miles away. Rome was now left mostly unprotected from threats to the east. The fiercest tribe, that of the Huns, was led by a warrior named Attila. He was especially known for his cruelty.

When Attila and his men advanced on Rome, Pope Leo the Great (452) went out to meet them with a delegation of priests and people. He intended to convince Attila not to destroy the city. As they approached, Attila saw a vision of Saints Peter and Paul on either side of the pope. It was as if they were ready to defend the city. Stunned by the vision, the Huns agreed to leave Rome in peace.

Attila

The Fall of Rome

Just three years later, however, a tribe known as the Vandals did manage to sack the city of Rome. The empire in the west was continuously invaded by barbarian hordes. The Ostrogoths, Visigoths, Huns, Burgundians, Vandals, and Franks all attacked at various times. In 476 the Goths returned to Rome and conquered it completely. The western half of the Roman Empire was now finished. The eastern half, however, with its capital at Constantinople, would continue for almost a thousand years more.

Conversion of the Franks

Interestingly, some of those responsible for destroying the empire were now accepting its Christian faith. King Clovis of the Franks was baptized in 496. It was through the effort of missionaries and the influence of his Christian wife, Saint Clotilda, that he asked for baptism. Many Franks followed his example. In time, the land of the Franks, much of which we now know as France, became a center of Catholic faith and culture.

On the Record

"The followers of Jesus are few. Although they have been scattered throughout the world, they quickly gather other believers. [. . .] Persecution seems to multiply their numbers. No suffering can keep them from reaching the ends of the earth."

—Saint Augustine of Hippo

Clovis is Baptized

Clotilda

The Arian Heresy Again

While the Church was enduring the barbarian invasions, she also suffered from heretical teaching. The most widespread heresy of the fifth century was still Arianism. Arians believed that Jesus was not God but a man chosen by God. The Councils of Nicea (325) and Constantinople (381) had condemned this false teaching, yet the Arians had spread their flawed version of Christianity to many migrating peoples in Europe. This complicated the Church's efforts. People already believed the Arian lies about Jesus. It was difficult to help them correct their errors and come into union with the Catholic faith.

Patrick

Brigid

Mystery of History

Where did Saint Patrick (389–461), the Apostle of Ireland, come from? It's unclear. We do know that, as a teenager, Patrick was kidnapped and brought to Ireland as a slave. There Patrick's faith deepened and became the center of his life. Eventually he escaped and was able to return home.

Patrick later became a priest. In 432 he went back to Ireland, this time as a missionary. Patrick inspired many people, including a holy woman named Brigid of Kildare (450–525). She became one of the founders of monastic life in Ireland; today she is known as Saint Brigid.

Thousands of people became Catholic because of Patrick's example and preaching. But no one really knows where he was born. Was Patrick English, Italian, or from some other country?

Tradition holds that young Patrick tended sheep herds on Slemish when he was held as a slave.

When we think of *nature,* we imagine the natural beauty of created things, like trees, flowers, animals, and insects. Another meaning of the word nature, though, refers to what makes a thing what it is and not something else. For example, a hippopotamus cannot be anything else but a hippo. It has the nature of a hippo and not of any other animal. We have a human nature, which means we can only be human beings. We are not merely animals, nor can we become angels.

Jesus, however, has the divine nature of God and a human nature from Mary. He is one person with two natures. He is *both* fully God *and* fully human. This is one of the great mysteries of our Catholic faith.

Christians have always believed and taught that Jesus Christ was the Son of God who became a human being to save us. It took many years, however, for the Church to explain exactly what that meant and how it was possible. In the fifth century, the Church held two councils: the Council of Ephesus (431) and the Council of Chalcedon (451). They confirmed the belief that Jesus Christ was one person with two natures. These councils were important for the Church's understanding of who Jesus Christ truly is. We call this understanding *Christology.*

Nestorius and the Mother of God

Another serious problem soon faced the Church. This time it came from Nestorius, the Bishop of Constantinople. He was teaching that Jesus had two natures—human and divine—but was also *two persons*—again, human and divine. Nestorius further taught that Mary was not the Mother of God. According to him, she was only mother of the human part of Jesus. The Council of Ephesus (431) condemned this teaching. It stated that Jesus is only one divine person with two natures that cannot be separated. And it declared Mary to be the Mother of God, or *Theotokos* ("Godbearer"). Nestorius accepted the authority of the council. The faith emerged clearer, stronger, and more unified than ever.

SNAPSHOT

Saint Jerome

Saint Jerome (340–420) was born near Dalmatia, on the coast of today's Croatia. After studying in Rome, he became a priest. Paintings often show him writing in a cave, sometimes with a lion nearby. It is true that Jerome spent time in a desert meditating and praying, but he was also a scholar.

For many years Jerome worked to translate the Bible from the original Hebrew and Greek languages into Latin. Latin was the official, and most common language of the Roman Empire at the time. He wrote commentaries on the faith, but his greatest love was the Bible. Jerome even moved to the Holy Land to be close to the places where the events of the Bible had occurred.

Jerome joined a monastery in Bethlehem. A group of Roman women often came, and he became their spiritual guide. Together they studied the Scriptures and discussed God's word. Several of these women also became saints: Paula, Marcella, Melania, and Eustochium.

Because his great contribution to biblical study had this significant impact on Christian teaching, Saint Jerome was named a doctor of the Church.

LATEST & GREATEST

The earliest known mechanism for processing cotton was invented in fifth-century India. A type of primitive cotton gin was created. A simple roller made of iron or wood was rolled over the cotton pods on a flat stone or wooden platform. The roller caused the seeds to pop out of their pod. Then the cotton fibers were gathered to be spun into thread and woven into cotton cloth.

Heresy and Schism

The confusion caused by these and other heretical teachings, however, did lead to major conflicts between church leaders. At times, large groups of Christians cut themselves off from the Church because they did not accept one of the council teachings. Sometimes these *schismatics* (skiz-MA-tiks) disputed the authority of the council or a bishop who had made the decisions. One of these groups was the Coptic Christians, who still live primarily in Egypt. They became a separate church after the Council of Chalcedon in 451.

The heretics and schismatics of this period were not bad Christians or bad people. Many, in fact, were theologians or bishops. Most of them were sincere disciples of Jesus Christ who were trying to understand and spread the Gospel. They sought the truth about God, but they made serious errors along the way. Their mistakes separated them from true faith in Christ. It is important to understand that the Church identified heretics not to punish but to correct them. Pope Leo the Great (around 400–461) wrote a number of letters trying to explain what was incorrect in the teachings of the Monophysites, Nestorians, Pelagians, and other heretics of his time.

More than the Facts

Alchemy is an ancient "science" in which people attempted to make various elements turn into gold. By the year 400, people in Europe had set up laboratories hoping to produce it. Related to this was the search for the Philosopher's Stone and the Elixir of Life. The Philosopher's Stone was a legendary substance that would change common metals into precious metals. The Elixir of Life was a liquid potion; it was supposed to give immortality to whoever drank it. Of course the search for these imaginary objects failed. However, it eventually led to the modern science of chemistry.

ACTIVITY

Choose a book, movie, or story about something historical. Read it or watch it with a couple of friends or family members. When and where do the events take place? What are the similarities and differences between then and now? Share your thoughts and ideas. How would *you* tell the story of what happened? What would change if the story occurred today?

Prayer

We ask you, Lord of all nations, to keep everyone in the world true to you. Make us all humble before you, our God. Make us respectful toward one another. May our disagreements and misunderstandings be worked out peacefully. Give us all the grace to accept correction when we are in error, and to listen carefully to those who teach us our faith. Amen.

The Bigger Picture

In this time of mass migrations, missionaries went to bring the Gospel to different people. The Church recognized and appreciated the good values and practices present in these people's cultures. Today *inculturation* is the name we give this process of bringing the Gospel to people where they are. Eventually, all those who moved into the lands once ruled by the Roman Empire were evangelized. The Goths, the Huns, and the Slavs—all became valuable members of the Church. In time, Christian kings, bishops, and missionaries came from among these people to evangelize and enrich the whole world.

As the Church grew and spread, it became necessary to better organize its structure and customs. In the next century struggles would arise between the government and church authorities. Conflicts began as people debated who had more authority—the pope or the emperor.

Chapter 6

AD 512

AD 524

530—Denis the Short, a Roman abbot, invents the *anno domini* (AD) method of dating years. *Anno domini* means "in the year of our Lord"; it begins the year Jesus was thought to be born.

535—Stained glass windows are installed in St. Sophia, the great church of Constantinople. Stained glass will not become common in Western Europe for several more centuries.

AD 536

AD 548

552–Buddhism spreads to Japan.

AD 560

570—Muhammad is born at Mecca.

AD 572

581—The Sui Dynasty of China under Wen Ti begins; this dynasty introduces the system of competitive exams to enter civil service.

AD 584

593—Suiko reigns as empress of Japan.

AD 596

600 —China begins printing books.

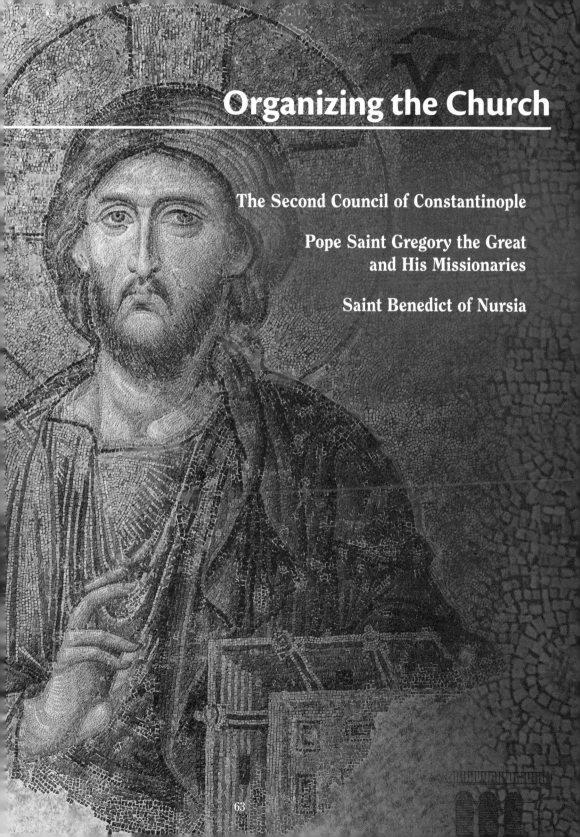

Organizing the Church

The Second Council of Constantinople

Pope Saint Gregory the Great
and His Missionaries

Saint Benedict of Nursia

When Justinian I (483–565) became emperor of Constantinople in 527, he saw the need to organize the empire. Spread over a vast area, it included many cultures with differing laws and customs. Justinian entrusted a lawyer with the task. Tribonian collected all the laws in effect at the time and organized them into official documents. By 533 the work, known as the Justinian Code, was finished. This code has influenced the laws of many great nations throughout history.

Justinian I

6th century

Theodora

The Second Council of Constantinople

Twenty years later, Justinian called the bishops to the Second Council of Constantinople (553). The pope at the time, Pope Vigilius (d. 557), was not in favor of a council. The emperor of the Eastern Empire, however, was powerful; he had the last say. Justinian's wife, Theodora, was a follower of Monophysitism, a heresy that claimed Jesus had only a divine nature and not a human one. The pope urged that this heresy be condemned, but the decisions of the council were not clear. In the end, neither the pope in Rome nor the emperor in Constantinople was satisfied. The divide between Christian leaders of the East and the West began.

LATEST & GREATEST

Stencils were used in China and Japan. Holes were pricked with a pin so that the outline of a design or a figure could be transferred to a copy. Ink was brushed over the pinholes, and the outlined image would appear under the stencil.

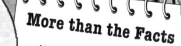

More than the Facts

Mercurius was the first pope to change his name. He did not think it was appropriate for a pope to keep the name of the pagan god Mercury, so he chose to be called Pope John II (533–535). Do you know Pope Francis' original name? How about the names of any other popes? Look at the list of popes on the downloadable PDF. Which names do you think are the most interesting?

On the Record

As emperor Justinian had his best scholars make a collection of Roman laws. They were organized into what was called the Justinian Code. Here is an example of one law:

"All nations agree that seashores are for public use, just as the sea itself is. Therefore, anyone can build a cottage as his home on the seashore, where he can dry his fishing nets and keep them safe from the water. The shores cannot be the property of any one person but are like the sea itself, the sand, and the ground beneath the sea."

Pope Saint Gregory the Great

Before he became pope, Gregory the Great (540–604) saw some children being sold as slaves in a city square. He learned they were children of the Angles, a tribe in the British Isles. *They look more like angels*, he thought. *I will volunteer to bring the Gospel to the Angles*. Unfortunately, Gregory was not able to go himself. But one of the first things he did when he became pope was send missionaries to Britain. He chose Augustine, a monk with a reputation for holiness. Augustine and his companions landed in 597. They worked tirelessly for the conversion of the people. Eventually, the whole kingdom of Kent (in southeast England) received Baptism. Today Augustine is known as Saint Augustine of Canterbury, the apostle of England.

Augustine

Columba

Pope Saint Gregory the Great and His Missionaries

Saint Gregory the Great (540–604) was elected pope in 590. Like Justinian, he too desired structure and reorganization. His focus, however, was the Church.

Gregory reformed the way the Church was governed and administered. He influenced the celebration of the liturgy and is credited with inspiring Gregorian chant. This is a form of music used in singing various psalms and prayers. Gregory also sent out missionaries to spread the Gospel to the far reaches of the empire. Among his missionaries were Saint Augustine of Canterbury (d. 605), who evangelized the Anglo-Saxons of Britain and was named the Archbishop of Canterbury; Saint David, who preached the Gospel in Wales; and Saint Columba (521–597), also known as Saint Columbkille, who converted the clans of Scotland. Saint Columba also began a monastery on the isle of Iona. This monastery was famous for training missionaries; many of them later became martyrs.

"Hello! My name is Kevin. I wanted to go with Brother Brendan on his voyage. He built an ox-hide boat with a mast and sails. Fourteen monks sailed away with him this morning. At the last minute, three unbelievers joined them. They are searching for paradise, the Isle of the Blessed. Hopefully, they won't find any sea monsters! I'm sure I'm strong enough to row, so I volunteered to go along. They left me behind, though, because Brother Brendan said I'm too young. I'm disappointed, but at least Brother Brendan said he thought I would be ready for his next trip."

Mystery of History

Did Saint Brendan sail to North America? Some people think so. Brendan the Navigator (486–575) was an Irish monk. He founded a monastery at Clonfert in 559. He was also well known for his missionary travels within Ireland and to Scotland. Was he really such a proficient seafarer to have crossed the Atlantic? Did he discover the North American continent? Where would he have landed?

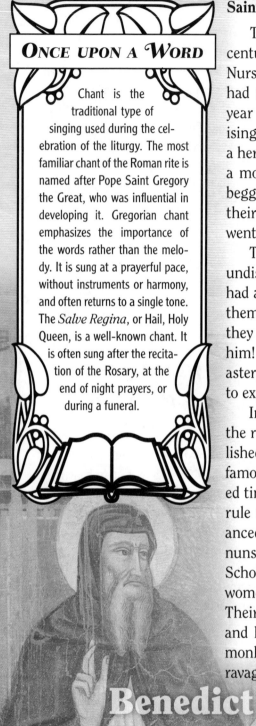

ONCE UPON A WORD

Chant is the traditional type of singing used during the celebration of the liturgy. The most familiar chant of the Roman rite is named after Pope Saint Gregory the Great, who was influential in developing it. Gregorian chant emphasizes the importance of the words rather than the melody. It is sung at a prayerful pace, without instruments or harmony, and often returns to a single tone. The *Salve Regina*, or Hail, Holy Queen, is a well-known chant. It is often sung after the recitation of the Rosary, at the end of night prayers, or during a funeral.

Saint Benedict of Nursia

The most important person of the sixth century may have been Saint Benedict of Nursia (480–550). As a young man Benedict had felt a great need for prayer. About the year 500, he gave up his wealth and a promising future in order to live alone in a cave as a hermit. In the same area of Italy there was a monastery without an abbot. The monks begged Benedict to lead them. Receiving their request as a call from God, Benedict went to live with them.

The monks turned out to be unruly and undisciplined. Soon they were sorry they had asked for Benedict; he was too strict for them. The monks were so disturbed that they even tried, unsuccessfully, to poison him! Benedict left and started his own monastery. It attracted so many members it had to expand to twelve locations.

In 529 Benedict went to Monte Cassino, the ruins of a pagan temple. There he established a large new monastery. He wrote his famous rule of life for monks, which included time for both prayer and work. Benedict's rule taught many how to live holy and balanced lives. He also began monasteries of nuns with the help of his twin sister, Saint Scholastica. This great band of men and women became known as the Benedictines. Their monasteries became beacons of light and learning for all of Europe. Benedictine monks helped re-evangelize Europe after the ravages of the barbarian invasions.

Benedict

Scholastica

ACTIVITY

If you were founding a monastery, what would your rule of life be like? How much time would your brothers or sisters spend in prayer? At work? At rest? What kind of abbot or abbess would you be? How would your community gain new members? Write a rule of life for yourself that you could live now. Try it for a day!

Prayer

Thank you, God, for the gift of organization. Sometimes I am not as organized as I should be. I misplace things; I lose time; I hurry through subjects and then can't remember what I studied. Help me to appreciate the mind you gave me and use it well. Teach me how to make time for work, play, and prayer. Amen.

The Bigger Picture

With Benedict, the first of the great religious orders in the West came into being at just the right moment of history. Many men and women would feel called to follow in Saint Benedict's footsteps and make his spirit of prayer and work (*ora et labora*) their own. The Church calls this spirit a *charism*. A charism is an inspiration given by God to an individual who then shares that gift with others so that it becomes a living treasure in the Church.

From the time of their founding, Benedictines have helped protect and enliven culture. In their *scriptoria*, or copy rooms, they wrote down many great books of the past. In this way the monks preserved these writings and made them available to the world. The Benedictines served as a model for other religious orders to follow. All use their charisms to help people know, love, and serve God and serve one another in charity.

In the coming century we will see how important it is to recognize and follow the inspirations of God. Tensions were growing between East and West, and between the Church and civil society. Sixth-century organization helped preserve order. It also raised questions about who had, or should have, the most power. Competing claims would not be resolved for several centuries. In the meantime, misunderstandings and conflicts would continue to challenge the Church.

Chapter 7

AD 610 — 610—Muhammad has a vision, sending him to preach.
He establishes the Islamic religion.

618—T'ang dynasty rules China.

AD 620 — 619—Persians take over Jerusalem.

AD 630

635—Chinese Emperor T'ai Tsung receives Christian missionaries.

638—Muslims capture Jerusalem and Syria.

AD 640 — 642—Egypt and all North Africa become Muslim.

AD 650

655—The Arab fleet defeats the Byzantine fleet off the Alexandrian coast.

AD 660

AD 670

AD 680

AD 690 — 690—Wu Zetian becomes Empress Wu, the only Chinese woman emperor
in history.

Trouble from Without and Within

Christianity Spreads in England

The Easter Controversy

Third Council of Constantinople

Saint Bathilde

Saint Benedict Biscop

The most significant event of the seventh century was the birth and spread of the Islamic religion. It was 610. Muhammad, who had been born in the Arabian city of Mecca, was forty years old. He believed he had a vision from God who told him to begin preaching. At first the people of Mecca did not take kindly to his new religion. They forced Muhammad to flee to Medina. (Mecca and Medina are cities in what is now Saudi Arabia.) There Muhammad began to attract followers to Islam. The most important beliefs Muhammad preached were that there is no god but Allah, that Allah has no son, and that Muhammad is his prophet.

Over the course of a few years, the new religion became more of a military campaign. The Muslims, as the followers of Muhammad came to be known, set out to conquer vast regions of the world. Within the century they had taken over Jerusalem and Syria, Egypt, and all of North Africa. Sadly, people were not given a choice of whether or not to convert to Islam. Many Christians and others chose to die rather than to convert to Islam. Some, however, converted out of fear. Or they did so hoping that it would be only temporary.

Muhammad died in 632. Since he did not have a son, Islamic believers disagreed over who should lead them. Muhammad's father-in-law, Abu Bakr, succeeded him as leader. But many believers decided instead to follow Ali, Muhammad's son-in-law. This split created the two main branches of Islam: Sunni and Shiite. The two factions have been at war and at peace in different periods of history.

century 7th

Mystery of History

In a village near Cambridge, England, the seventh-century burial site of an Anglo-Saxon teenage girl was discovered. Historians are intrigued, since she was found buried in her bed (in the grave) and had a solid gold and garnet cross on her clothing. To be buried with something so valuable, she must have been someone of importance. But who? Was she a princess? And how did she die?

Christianity Spreads in England

Losing North Africa and much of the Holy Land was painful for Christianity. Still, there were also many wonderful signs of hope for the Church. Missionaries continued to preach the Gospel. Two notable examples are Saint Paulinus of York and Saint Aidan of Ireland. Both men worked to convert Northumbria, or northern England.

King Edwin of Northumbria won a battle for Wessex in 627. Afterward, he requested Baptism from Paulinus. Paulinus was then able to preach the Gospel freely throughout the king's territory.

In 640, King Oswald called for Saint Aidan from the monastery of Iona. The king asked him to strengthen Christianity in Northumbria. Aidan brought his version of faith in Christ. It was known as Celtic Christianity. Certain Celtic Christian practices were unique and different from the Roman Christianity familiar to the rest of England and most of Christian Europe.

Oswald

Aidan

ONCE UPON A WORD

The way in which a sacrament or religious ceremony is carried out is known as a *rite*. Each sacrament that we celebrate has its own rite: the rite of Baptism, the rite of Confirmation, etc. Rite may also refer to a group of Christian churches within the Catholic Church who have preserved ancient rituals, discipline, and customs. The largest number of Catholics are Roman Catholics. Other Catholics, however, belong to various other rites: West Syrian, Armenian, Byzantine, East Syrian, and Alexandrian. These Catholics recognize the authority of the pope, but they have their own bishops. Sometimes they even have patriarchs, or chief bishops. The Catholic Church is actually made up of more than twenty distinct churches!

The Easter Controversy

One of the differences was the date set for Easter. The Celts used one calculation, while the Romans used another. This caused confusion, especially when neighbors followed different traditions. For example, the next king, Oswy, was a Celtic Catholic. His queen was a Roman Catholic, as was his son. Because of this, part of the royal family was still observing the Lenten fast while others were celebrating Easter.

In 664, the king called a meeting at the monastery of Whitby to discuss the problem. The king allowed the bishop to explain the Celtic view, which he claimed came from Saint John the Apostle. Saint Wilfred explained the Roman view, which he claimed came from Saint Peter. King Oswy then asked the assembly: "Do we all agree that Peter is the prince of the Apostles?" They all said they did. "Then we will follow the traditions of the Roman Church," he declared.

This decision essentially caused all of England to adopt the practices of Roman Catholicism. It signaled the end of many distinctive Celtic Catholic practices. Diversity was largely welcomed in the Church, but not at the cost of unity.

Wilfred

"My name is Youssef and I'm a Maronite. I'm on my way to the holy liturgy. Did you know we pray in a language very similar to the one Jesus spoke? We speak Syriac, which is a form of Aramaic. Our new patriarch, John Maroun, will celebrate today. This is a special time to be a Maronite. We haven't had a leader since the patriarch of Antioch was martyred about eighty years ago. But now we have our own Maronite patriarch. Yes, we are loyal to the pope. But we go back to when the followers of Jesus in Antioch were first called Christians. In the fourth century we were organized as an Eastern Catholic rite by a monk named Marun. We really are part of the ancient Church."

I Witness

Third Council of Constantinople

A few years later, in 680, bishops met a third time in Constantinople. This time they assembled to resolve the Monothelite heresy. Monothelitism taught that Jesus was not fully human; that he had no human will but only a divine will. According to true belief, Jesus is *both* fully human and fully divine. He is one divine person with two wills, human and divine. The Third Council of Constantinople was yet another occasion for Church leaders to come together and defend the Christian teachings against error. The Councils built and demonstrated the bishops' unity in Christ.

Marun

Saint Bathilde

Throughout the Church's story there have been wonderful examples of holiness. Two of the most outstanding figures from the 600s are Saint Bathilde (died in 680) and Saint Benedict Biscop (628–689).

Bathilde began life as a slave in the Frankish kingdom of Clovis II. When Clovis caught sight of Bathilde's beauty and learned of her wisdom and kindness, he fell in love with her. He freed Bathilde from slavery in 649, then married her. The couple had three sons before his early death in 656.

Bathilde then became regent, that is, she ruled in the place of her eldest son until he was old enough to be king. During her reign she performed many charitable works; she also gave order to civil and church life. Bathilde abolished slavery and ended the corrupt practice of buying and selling church favors. When her sons were of age, she retired to the monastery she had founded near Paris. There she took a lowly position, spending her days in prayer and modest service. In the course of her lifetime, Bathilde went from being a slave to a queen to a humble religious.

More than the Facts

Saint Isidore, bishop of Seville (around 560–636), is a patron saint of the Internet. This may seem unusual; after all, he lived many centuries before the age of electronics. Isidore, however, possessed a vast store of knowledge. He really was the "computer geek" of his day. Isidore wrote books on mathematics, logic, history, medicine, philosophy, theology, grammar, and public speaking. He also wanted bishops to establish schools in their dioceses. Isidore knew that education was the way to progress.

SNAPSHOT

Caedmon

Caedmon (d. 680) cared for the animals of the abbey at Whitby, England; he did not seem to have any other talents. While everyone else took turns in the evening telling stories and singing songs, Caedmon went back to his animals. One night a man appeared in Caedmon's dream and asked him to sing. To his own surprise, when Caedmon tried he actually composed a poem-song. The next evening he sang this poem-song, which was about creation. In time he added other biblical stories to his song. Only a few verses of his writing have been preserved. However, Caedmon is honored as the earliest known English poet. Here is a translation of a few lines of *Caedmon's Hymn*:

Praise now the Lord of heaven's kingdom,
the Creator's power and his will.
The glorious Father's heart
tells how for each wonderful work,
the eternal One set the start.

On the Record

Pope Agatho (678–681) and one hundred twenty-five bishops of the West met together in Rome. Afterward they sent a profession of faith to the Third Council of Constantinople (680–681). They realized they were late sending the document. The pope apologized to Emperor Constantine IV and the bishops assembled in council. Agatho explained how difficult it had been getting everyone together for the meeting:

"First of all, many had to come from great distances, even from the coast. Because of the distance, their travel took a long time. We also hoped that our brother Bishop Theodore, the archbishop and philosopher of Great Britain, and others who were there for a long time, could come. We wanted this document we are sending to represent our fellow believers, who labor among the Longobards, the Sclavi, the Franks, the French, the Goths, and the Britons. [. . .] They constantly inquire about what is being done in the cause of the apostolic faith."

Saint Benedict Biscop

Saint Benedict Biscop was a landholder connected to the king of Northumbria in northern England. He decided to become a monk and traveled to Rome. While there he was introduced to Wilfrid, who was also from Northumbria. Wilfrid was a monk and a bishop about to be sent to England. His superiors had asked him to promote the liturgy and practices of the Roman Church. Benedict gladly returned as Wilfrid's companion.

In 668 Benedict again went to Rome. He wanted to learn more about how the Church operates. When he returned to England, he was appointed abbot of a monastery in Canterbury. Several years later, he introduced a new building style for churches. He had learned the style from the stone churches in France and Rome. It included glass windows. In fact, Benedict was the first to introduce glass windows to England!

This innovative monk died at the age of sixty-two in Wearmouth, Northumbria. He is honored for the beauty and grace he brought to the English church. Benedict is often called the "Father of Benedictines in England."

Saint Augustine Abbey

LATEST & GREATEST

The game of chess probably originated in India. The first figures used were primitive carvings. Arab traders introduced chess to the people of Europe. But Arabs had their own game, too. You may have heard of it. Have you ever played backgammon?

ACTIVITY

Learn about the different rites within the Catholic Church. If one of these rites has a parish in your area, attend liturgy there or go to visit.

Prayer

God, my Father, many people in your world are not Christians. I pray that we can love and respect one another as your children. I pray also that those who are not Christian will respect my faith in your Son, Jesus. Help us live together in peace, and work together to make the world a safe and welcoming place for everyone. Amen.

The Bigger Picture

Did you know that there are two other great religions beside Christianity that believe in one God? Neither Muslims nor Jews believe in the Holy Trinity. However, the followers of both Judaism and Islam believe that there is only one God. In our world there are many, many religions in which people sincerely believe. As Christians we cannot agree that religions are equally true, or that practicing any set of beliefs is fine. Still, practicing our faith means treating everyone with respect. We need to act as the children of our loving God and Father.

In the chapters ahead, we will learn about the many challenges of living with people of different religions or no religion. We will see the conflicts that brought about wars and suffering. As we study these past events, we can learn from them. Admitting our sins, mistakes, and failings can help us to write a better story of the Church and the world in the future.

Chapter 8

AD 710

711—Muslims invade Spain and overthrow Spain's last Visigoth king.

716—Muslims conquer Lisbon, Portugal.

AD 720

717–Islamic forces besiege Constantinople, but do not succeed in taking over.

AD 730

732—Charles Martel leads the Frankish army in defeat of the Arabs and confines them south of the Pyrenees Mountains.

AD 740

AD 750

750—Baghdad, now the capital of Iraq, becomes the capital of the Islamic Empire.

752—The Papacy breaks free from the dominating power of the Byzantine emperor.

AD 760

756—Pepin the Short protects Pope Stephen II from the Lombards. The lands conquered by Pepin are donated to the pope and become known as the Papal States.

AD 770

AD 780

AD 790

800—Charlemagne is crowned first emperor of the Holy Roman Empire.

Darkness and Light

The years from AD 500 to 1000 are often referred to as the Dark Ages. The great Roman Empire had collapsed. The government, court system, military defense—the things most people take for granted—no longer functioned. Between 537 and 752, all of the popes came from the Byzantine Empire. And every pope's election had to be approved by the Byzantine emperor. There were ups and downs all over the globe. In China the Tang Dynasty was thriving. In the Middle East and in Europe, Muslims were expanding their influence. But the glorious Mayan civilization of South America was already in decline.

The Roman Empire's weak structure, and the constant fear of war, put any growth of culture and learning on hold for the next five hundred years. Still, despite the fear and uncertainty of this period, the eighth century was a time of holiness and charity. In fact, for the Church it was a time of *light in darkness*. Three saints stand out in particular as bright lights during this century.

sculpture of a woman from the Tang Dynasty

8th century

Mayan Zodiac Circle

Saint Bede

The first "light" of the eighth century was Saint Bede (673–735); he is often called Bede the Venerable. Bede was one of the most educated men of his time. At the age of seven, he was placed in a local monastery in order to receive a good education. At seventeen, he took religious vows and became a monk of the Wearmouth-Jarrow Abbey of Northumberland, England.

Bede is best known as the author of the *Ecclesiastical* (or Church) *History of the English People*. In this work he tells us that he relied on many former accounts of historical events; he also used the collected memories of others. His book was the first history of the Church in Britain. It is a valuable source of knowledge about early worship and organization of Church life. Bede's history helped popularize the use of BC and AD to place events in relation to the birth of Christ. The saint also wrote Scripture commentaries, a book on chant, biographies, and numerous letters. His life was spent teaching, studying, and writing. Pope Leo XIII declared him a doctor of the Church in 1899.

Bede

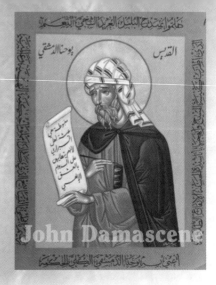

John Damascene

Saint John Damascene

The second saint we remember from this century is Saint John Damascene (675–749). John's first career was as a civil official in the service of the caliph, the Muslim civil leader of Damascus, Syria. But in 716, John entered the monastery of Saint Sabas in Jerusalem. He became a renowned opponent of the *iconoclasts* (eye-KON-o-klasts). These heretics believed that the commandment against idolatry forbade religious images of any kind. Supported by Byzantine Emperor Leo III, they tried to rid the Church of all icons and other sacred images of Jesus, Mary, the saints, and angels. Saint John dedicated his life to combating their false teachings. The Church adopted John's work as the official teaching about icons and images at the Second Council of Nicea in 787. John also wrote a summary of the works of the great Greek theologians. He composed many hymns used even today to praise God. Saint John Damascene is considered the last of the Greek Fathers of the Church.

Saint Boniface

Our third saint was a hands-on evangelizer. Saint Boniface (680–754) was a missionary bishop from England. Pope Gregory II sent him to Germany, and later to France, to preach the Gospel. For forty years Boniface used his practical skills and friendly character to convert people to the Catholic faith. Many came from pagan religions; many more had accepted the errors of Arian Christianity. Boniface helped them all.

Boniface founded monasteries and dioceses. In 747 he was made archbishop of Germany. A few years later, in 754, Boniface was with a group of Confirmation candidates for a Pentecost eve celebration. Suddenly a horde of barbarians attacked. Boniface and his companions were martyred. This ultimate sacrifice in service to Christ was the crowning glory of his life as a missionary. Today Boniface is recognized as the patron saint of Germany.

On the Record

Here is part of a letter from Saint Boniface (680–754), the apostle of Germany, to the abbot of Wearmouth-Jarrow Abbey in England:

"I, Boniface, a humble servant of the servants of God, send a brotherly greeting in Christ to my dear, revered brother, Abbot Huetbert, and to all the brothers of his holy community.

"Please, dear brother, assist us in our work with your holy prayers. We labor to sow the seed of the Gospel among the rough and savage people of Germany.

". . . Meanwhile, would you make a copy to send me of the writings of Bede the monk? We have heard that he is a brilliant student of the Scriptures and a light within the Church.

"If possible, would you also send me a cloak? That would be a real comfort on my journeys."

Boniface

Pepin

Martel

The Battle of Tours

Throughout the eighth century, Muslim warriors continued their conquest of nations. It did not take long for them to cross the sea from North Africa and advance into Spain. Once there, Muslim forces were positioned to invade the rest of Europe. But they were met and defeated in France by Charles Martel (called "the Hammer") at the Battle of Tours in 732.

Europe grew stronger under Martel's son Pepin (714–768), who was known as Pepin the Younger or Pepin the Short. Pepin continued his father's campaigns against Islamic forces attempting to overtake Europe. He supported the papacy and gave the pope land that later became the Papal States. Pepin was crowned king of the Franks. He was the founder of the Carolingian dynasty, which ruled most of Europe from 751 until 987.

More than the Facts

Chang'an was the capital of the Tang Dynasty in China; it was the largest city in the world during this century. Chang'an had a million inhabitants. There was an equal number of people in the surrounding areas. The city boasted a zoo, public parks, and gardens.

Mystery of History

In present-day Cahokia, Illinois there are many large mounds on which ancient peoples built their dwellings. These mounds also contain burial remains. Who were the people who developed a civilization there? What caused them to disappear from history? A circular pattern of wooden poles was also found in the area. It resembles the structure at Stonehenge in England. Was this for ceremonial or scientific use? Mystery surrounds the entire site.

"My name is Mikael. I am *writing* an icon. Yes, it looks like I am painting, but an icon is a very special religious image. We *write* the meaning in the symbols we use and by the poses we give our subjects. We pray and fast for inspiration, too. My icon is simple because I'm just learning, but there are many beautiful icons, especially in the churches of the East. Now that the Church council has decided to restore the holy images, I'll have a lot of work to do."

I Witness

SNAPSHOT

Leoba

Among the remarkable people who lived in the eighth century was a nun named Leoba (around 710–779).

When she was only seven years old, Leoba's parents placed her in the monastery of Wimborne, England, to be educated. She spent her time well in the various duties of her religious life, but she gave special attention to her studies.

Leoba became a biblical scholar and an expert on the writings of the Fathers of the Church. When her cousin, Saint Boniface, needed helpers for his missionary work among the Germanic people, he asked for Leoba. She proved a perfect choice.

For forty years Leoba served among the Germanic people. She was a favorite of Charlemagne and his wife; she also advised church officials and monks.

Leoba died at her Bischofsheim monastery in 779. At her death, the people all considered her a saint.

Charlemagne

Pepin's son Charlemagne ruled next. On Christmas Day in the year 800, Pope Leo III crowned him king. Charlemagne became the first Holy Roman emperor of the West to be crowned at St. Peter's Basilica in Rome. By crowning Charlemagne, the pope gained military support for the Vatican. And Charlemagne (also known as Charles the Great) had the approval he needed to begin to reestablish unity in the Roman Empire in Europe.

Peace, however, would soon be shattered again. Viking Norsemen from Scandinavia had begun staging raids along the coast of Ireland and England. In 787 they brutally attacked and destroyed the monastery on the island of Lindisfarne. This was the first of many attacks on monasteries and churches. The Norsemen were intent on seizing the gold of the chalices and crosses. Their destruction deprived the Church of its centers of prayer and learning.

Charlemagne

... A PRIORI ...

LATEST & GREATEST

Charlemagne had many plans to advance his kingdom. He wanted to improve education and culture among his people. He brought Alcuin (735–804), a leading scholar from York, England, to his palace in Aachen, Germany. Together, the emperor and the scholar set up an education plan; it included a school for the clergy and schools of higher learning. By 802, Charlemagne had made a law requiring every town to have a primary school. The emperor, his wife, and his children all attended school at the palace. Alcuin directed the royal library and traveled extensively. He collected and copied various books. The books were then distributed widely within the empire.

ACTIVITY

Learn about missionaries from your own parish or diocese. Where is their mission? How long have they been there? Write a letter of encouragement and promise your prayers for the success of their evangelizing work.

the Vikings are coming!

Prayer

Lord, we ask you to bless all the missionaries of today. Give them the knowledge and compassion they need to plant the Gospel everywhere. Continue to inspire men and women to leave their own lands and go where you send them to preach the Good News. Show each one of us how to be missionaries of our faith right where we live. Amen.

The Bigger Picture

In the eighth century, difficulties between civil and church authorities grew more serious. The leader of the Church in the East, the patriarch of Constantinople, remained very much under the emperor's control. Things were better by the end of the century, however. The papacy was no longer under the shadow of the Byzantine emperor. But this also contributed to the growing division between the churches of the East and those of the West. The balance of power between the pope of Rome and the newly formed Holy Roman Empire was not yet clear.

A number of monasteries and other centers of culture were destroyed. But the Church remained a cultural force and guardian of learning. During this century of great unrest, the value of sacred art was clarified. Both eastern and western churches confronted the heresy of iconoclasm. Iconoclasts believed that images on the walls of churches and in books distracted people from true faith in God. They argued that Christians should concentrate on God in their hearts and in their prayer. In her wisdom, however, the Church insisted that images and icons help us to understand and be devoted to the God we cannot see. The Church's approval of sacred art would result in inspiring cultural achievements in the centuries to come. It would also make the Church the largest patron of the arts in history.

Chapter 9

800–900—The Mayan civilization is at its height on the Yucatán peninsula of Mexico. The large pyramid calendar of Kukulcan, now considered one of the New Seven Wonders of the World, is built at Chichén Itzá.

AD 812

AD 824

825—The remains of Saint James the Apostle are discovered, and the Shrine of Santiago de Compostela in Spain is built.

AD 836

AD 848

844—Kenneth MacAlpine, king of the Scots, conquers the Picts and unifies Scotland.

853—Vikings take over Ireland.

AD 860

862—Rurik the Viking seizes northern Russia.

868—In China, Buddhist monks at the monastic caverns of Tun-Huang print a version of *The Diamond Sutra*. (Metal, movable printing will be invented by Gutenberg in the 1400s.)

AD 872

875—Beginnings of medieval drama—perhaps a dramatization of the liturgy

880—Byzantine Emperor Basil recovers Italy from Arab forces.

AD 884

AD 896

899—Magyars from the East invade Moravia. They later mingle with other tribes and become the people we know as Hungarians.

900—Alfonso III begins the reconquest of Spain, slowly defeating the Muslims.

Conversions

As the ninth century opened, a group of Irish monks began a new life in Iceland. Early histories state that they actually landed in the Faeroe Islands near Iceland. By 825 the monks had been living there as hermits for nearly a hundred years. When the Vikings arrived in 874, ready to colonize the area, the monks fled to avoid being captured and enslaved.

the Faeroe Islands

9th century

Mystery of History

Who created the Book of Kells and where was it made?
The Book of Kells is an intricately illuminated manuscript of the four Gospels. It is believed to be the work of eighth- or ninth-century monks from one of Saint Columba's monasteries in Scotland. No one knows the book's origin for certain, however. Perhaps it was moved to the monastery in Kells, Ireland to save it from Viking raids. Each of the 680 individual pages of smooth calfskin vellum is illustrated with scenes from the Gospel or large ornamental letters to accompany the text. In the eleventh century the book was stolen and its cover was torn off. Scholars believe the original cover had been inlaid with gold and jewels. The book itself survived this attack. Over the years it has been divided into four separate volumes. Today they are safeguarded in the library of Trinity College in Dublin.

Louis the Pious

partible succession

Divided Kingdoms

Significant social changes began to develop in Europe. In 828, Charlemagne's son, Louis the Pious (778–840), divided his empire among his three eldest sons Lothair, Louis the German, and Pepin. When Pepin died in 838, Louis the Pious gave his youngest son, Charles the Bald, his brother's portion of the kingdom. This division of the empire was known as *partible succession*, or inheriting a part of the kingdom. It meant that the empire was broken up, first among sons and then among grandsons, until all that remained was a number of very small kingdoms. While this practice may have seemed like a fair thing to do, it ultimately weakened the Frankish Empire. In the following years, partible succession led to constant jealousy and warfare. This system subdivided the strength of the empire. It made it difficult to organize against the continual attacks from the Vikings.

LATEST & GREATEST

According to legend, goatherds in Ethiopia (around 850) noticed that their animals became lively after eating a certain berry. Because the pits inside tasted bitter, the men did not eat the berries themselves. Instead they tossed them into their fire. The aroma of the roasting seeds was wonderful. The goatherds eventually brewed some of the seeds in water, which created a pleasant, stimulating drink. It became known as *quawah*, which means "infusion." Later the drink was called *qahve*, from which we get "coffee."

The Feudal System

The feudal system was a related development during this century. It began among the Franks and spread across Europe. The feudal system grew out of partible succession, since the little kingdoms that were formed required their own governments, armies, workers, and so on.

In the feudal system there was a leader (a king or a prince), and under him were barons. Each baron had a number of knights in his service. They owed allegiance to the baron, who owed his allegiance to the king. The knights and their men fought for a baron, and the baron pledged these fighters to the king. In return for their service, kings gave land (known as *fiefs*) to the knights, who in turn gave land to their soldiers. At the bottom of the whole system were ordinary people, known as serfs or peasants. They did not own land. Serfs were farmers, shopkeepers, and common laborers. Although they did have some rights, serfs were not permitted to move about freely. They "belonged" to the land they worked, and indirectly to the person who owned that land.

More than the Facts

By the early 800s mathematicians of India began using zero as a numeral in their calculations. For centuries a circle or dot had been placed as a marker in math by many peoples of the world, including the advanced Olmec and Mayan civilizations of South America. The East Indians, however, integrated it as a value in multiplication, division, addition, and subtraction.

The Feudal System and the Church

The feudal system held countries together in this tumultuous time. It provided people with leadership and protection.

The Church was part of the feudal system. Bishops were landowners, as were monastic communities. They had to provide for themselves from the land. So bishops would divide their property among their soldiers and vassals, who would farm it in return for their military service. Unfortunately, this system often required bishops and abbots to lead armies to protect their land or to fight battles for the king.

In some parts of Europe the feudal system continued until the sixteenth century. In Russia, serfs did not become free until the nineteenth century.

Pope Saint Nicholas I

Nicholas was born in Italy around the year 800. When Pope Benedict III died in 858, Emperor Louis II insisted that Nicholas succeed him. The emperor had Nicholas consecrated and enthroned on the very day of his election. But the new pope proved to be stronger than the emperor had expected. For example, Pope Nicholas confronted the emperor when he wanted to divorce his wife and marry another woman. Nicholas also excommunicated Photius in 863, after he replaced Ignatius as patriarch of Constantinople. As chief shepherd, Nicholas challenged Bishop John of Ravenna as well. The bishop was oppressing his people, demanding large sums of money from them. He also imprisoned priests who opposed him. Because Bishop John did not listen to the pope, he was removed from office and eventually excommunicated. He was not the only one to be censured. Nicholas had to discipline other bishops and civil officials as well.

Nonetheless, Pope Nicholas put himself at the service of these same men as teacher and counselor. One example of his fatherly attention is seen in his interaction with Boris, king of Bulgaria. Boris was a new convert to Christianity. He needed help understanding the proper way to govern Christians who had been so recently pagans. Boris sent the pope a letter containing 106 questions! Pope Nicholas gladly replied to each one.

Many threats were being made against the Church's authority at that time. Nicholas did a lot to strengthen the papacy during a period of moral weakness. He is one of only three popes (along with Leo I and Gregory I) officially given the title "Great." He received this distinction because of his vigorous efforts to defend the faith and keep the Church strong. Pope Nicholas died on November 13, 867.

SNAPSHOT

Veni, Creator Spiritus

A German monk named Rabanus Maurus (776–856) gave the Church a great gift at the beginning of the ninth century. He composed the ancient and well-known hymn *Veni, Creator Spiritus* ("Come, Creator Spirit"). Rabanus Maurus was just one example of the fervor and dedication found in the monks of his time. Maurus was a learned man. He was a Scripture scholar who had studied under Alcuin (732–804), the scholar who helped Charlemagne found a school at Aachen. Maurus became abbot of the monastery Saint Boniface founded at Fulda, in what is now Germany. Later, as archbishop of Mainz, Maurus became known for his preaching and works of charity.

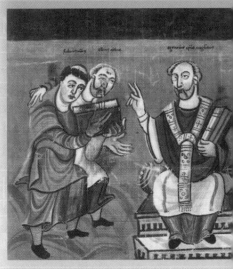

Rabanus Maurus, supported by Alcuin, dedicates his work to Archbishop Otgar of Mainz

"My name is Nika, and I am learning to write the new alphabet that Father Cyril gave us here in Moravia. He said it matches our spoken language better than the Western Latin alphabet or the Greek one. When Father Cyril arrived here, we Slavs were new Christians. He and his brother Methodius came as missionaries and teachers. They realized that we would learn more quickly if we had the Scriptures in our own language. So Father Cyril created this alphabet. Together both priests translated the Bible and the liturgy into a language we can understand. I am eager to hear these holy words for myself. But first I have over forty letters to learn, so I had better say goodbye and get back to my studies."

I Witness

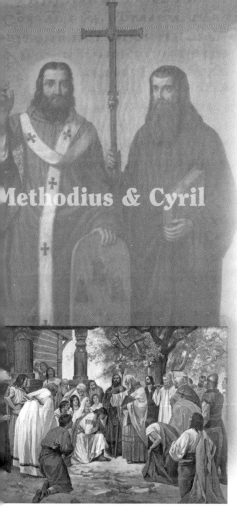

Methodius & Cyril

Saints Cyril and Methodius

The Holy Spirit was at work in many missionaries. Two of the best known were Saint Cyril (826–869) and Saint Methodius (815–884). These two men were brothers. In 863 they were sent by the patriarch of Constantinople to evangelize the Slavic peoples. The Slavs, who originated in central Asia, were the last tribes to pour into Europe in mass migrations.

Prince Ratislav of Moravia requested someone to explain Sacred Scripture and teach him the Christian faith. The two brothers knew how to speak the Slavic language and, in time, created an alphabet for it. They translated the Gospels and the Acts of the Apostles into their new Cyrillic alphabet. With the pope's permission, they also celebrated the liturgy in Slavonic. Saints Cyril and Methodius are known as the apostles of the Slavs. Today they are co-patrons of Europe, together with Saint Benedict of Nursia.

Saint Ansgar

Another important missionary was the French Benedictine monk, Saint Ansgar (801–865). He was sent to the lands of northern Europe. Ansgar went first to Denmark and then to Sweden, where he preached the Gospel with some success. Pope Nicholas I named Ansgar his personal representative to these northern countries as well as to Germany. Ansgar had to rebuild the church often, however, due to frequent invasions by pagan Norsemen.

Ansgar

Saint Edmund and the Vikings

Many fierce Norse warriors led large armies of followers throughout Europe. One such warrior, Ivar Ragnarsson (around 794–873), had a very unusual nickname: "the Boneless." No one knows why he was called "Boneless." Perhaps it was because he was so agile that he seemed to have no bones!

The Viking Ivar was tall and powerful. He was leader of the terrifying Great Heathen Army, which eventually conquered all of Britain. Among Ivar's conquests was the kingdom of East Anglia. In a battle that occurred in 865, East Anglia's King Edmund was captured and brutally murdered. Because he never stopped blessing the name of Jesus during his sufferings, he is known as Saint Edmund the Martyr. The place of his martyrdom became a shrine known for miracles and cures.

By 871 Ivar had made his way to Dublin. He reigned there as king until his death. Ivar was succeeded by one of his brothers, who was not as successful in battle as he had been. In fact, the Irish managed to drive the Vikings from Dublin by 902. Although Vikings raided Ireland until the middle of the tenth century, this was the beginning of their ultimate defeat in the British Isles.

Edmund

Alfred found much pleasure in reading

Alfred disguised himself and entered the Danish camp

On the Record

King Alfred the Great of England (849–899) wanted to rebuild his kingdom after the Vikings' terrible destruction. He did for England what Charlemagne had done in Germany: he developed schools and encouraged learning. Alfred translated a number of important books on history and philosophy from Latin into English. These included Pope Gregory's *Pastoral Care* and the works of Boethius (a Roman senator and philosopher), Orosius (a theologian and student of Saint Augustine), and Saint Bede. The king wanted to continue the account Bede had begun in his *Ecclesiastical History.* So Alfred commissioned the writing of the Anglo-Saxon *Chronicle,* one of the first histories of England, in 891.

He wrote the following in his preface to *Pastoral Care:*

"[. . .] I seriously wondered why the good and wise men who lived throughout England in times past, and who knew all these books well, had not translated them into their own language. But the answer came to me immediately: They never imagined that men would become so careless or that learning would be so abandoned. They purposely refrained, thinking the more languages we knew the more wisdom would exist in our land."

No Council to Decide

Meanwhile, tension continued to mount between the East and the West. In 858 the Byzantine Emperor Michael III removed the patriarch of Constantinople from office. In his place the emperor appointed a layman named Photius. Michael III was angry that Pope Nicholas I had allowed Eastern Catholic churches to celebrate the liturgy the way Roman Catholics did.

There was also disagreement over the Latin word *filioque* in the Nicene Creed. The word *filioque* means "and the Son." In its teaching about the Holy Trinity, the Roman Church said that the Holy Spirit comes from both the Father *and* the Son. The Eastern Church, instead, believed that the Holy Spirit came from the Father alone. Normally a council would have been called to settle this type of disagreement. However, the Church in the West decided to change the ancient creed without consulting the Eastern Church. The Roman Church went ahead and added *filioque* to the Nicene Creed. Unfortunately, that act damaged the unity of faith which the creed was written to create and protect.

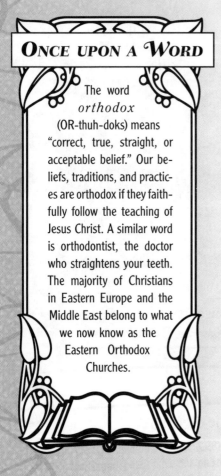

ONCE UPON A WORD

The word *orthodox* (OR-thuh-doks) means "correct, true, straight, or acceptable belief." Our beliefs, traditions, and practices are orthodox if they faithfully follow the teaching of Jesus Christ. A similar word is orthodontist, the doctor who straightens your teeth. The majority of Christians in Eastern Europe and the Middle East belong to what we now know as the Eastern Orthodox Churches.

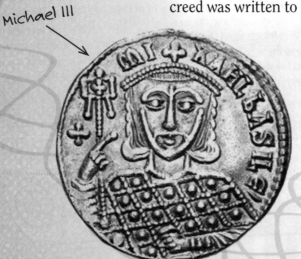

Michael III

ACTIVITY

King Alfred the Great asked monks to perfect a wax candle that would burn for exactly twenty-four hours as a way to keep track of time. These became known as calibrated candles. Look up some of the ways people have kept time over the centuries. Sundials, hourglasses, and clocks have interesting stories behind them!

Prayer

Dear Lord, help me to learn from the people and events of history to live in peace every day of my life. Teach me to look for ways to understand and respect the differences among people. Let me welcome everyone in your name. Amen.

The Bigger Picture

Culture and learning flourished in the West during the ninth century. This was largely due to Charlemagne's efforts. He created libraries and made books more widely available. Even though valuable resources were being lost in violent attacks, new collections were always being formed. Most importantly, the emperor founded schools to teach people how to read. He instilled in others an eagerness to learn.

The practice of partible succession led to a constant struggle among rulers for dominance. This ultimately weakened the nations in Europe. Meanwhile, invading Vikings gained ground, taking over whole kingdoms. In fact, the largest number of Viking invasions of Britain happened between the years 856 and 875. Vikings conquered Ireland in 853 and ruled there until 1014.

These were years of fragmentation in the great empires. Instead of the strength and wisdom of large, unified countries, division and subdivision of kingdoms continued, and new kingdoms were formed. The Church struggled to maintain the presence of Christ, and his influence, among the people. But change was also coming to the Church. Rather than learning from the fragmenting of kingdoms around her, the Christian Church was heading for division between the East and the West.

Chapter 10

Age of Kings

With the breaking up of kingdoms and the threats against the one true Church, many attempts were made to bring about unity. In the year 910, an influential movement began among the Benedictine monasteries of Europe. The duke of Aquitaine and a monk, Saint Berno, founded the abbey of Cluny in Burgundy, France. Under succeeding abbots, Cluny became a model monastery. By the end of the tenth century, more than a thousand monasteries were under the direction of the abbot of Cluny. This alliance of monasteries demonstrated a strengthening of commitment to religious life in the Church.

Cluny

10th century

Charles III.

he was known as Charles the Simple or the Straightforward

Rollo's baptism and marraige to Gisela

Changes in Western Europe

Meanwhile, changes were taking place in Europe. At the beginning of the century, Edward, known as the Elder, became king of two dominant peoples of Britain, the Angles and the Saxons. Thirty-five years later, Aethelstan defeated an alliance of all the other people of the British Isles to become king of all Britain. In France, King Charles III granted feudal lands to the Viking Rollo in order to promote peace for his people. Rollo was later baptized Christian and took the name Robert. With this grant, the once fierce Norsemen became the Normans.

receuou baptefme lon
aultnent qui lui don
neroit Gille fa fille
par mariage et toute
la terre De la cuuete de

Comment Rollo receut

Social Changes around the World

Changes also took place in other parts of the world during this century. Among them were the beginnings of the New Zealand settlement by the Maori of Polynesia; the invasion of German lands by the Magyars (known today as the Hungarians); the civil war that brought the great Chinese Tang Dynasty to an end and allowed the Mongols to begin invading the northern parts of China; the founding of Korea; the emergence of Poland as a nation under the rule of Mieszko I; the settlement of the Arabs along the eastern coast of Africa; the settlement of Greenland by Vikings from Iceland; and the sighting of the new land of North America by the same Vikings.

Mieszko I

Mystery of History

Did the Viking Leif Erikson discover North America in the year 1000? Was the settlement found in 1963 at L'Anse aux Meadows in Newfoundland really the place where he landed?

Leif Erikson was born somewhere between 960 and 980 in a Viking settlement in Greenland. His father was Erik the Red, a Viking from Norway. When Leif traveled to Norway, he converted to Christianity and was sent back to Greenland by King Olaf I. The king sent priests with Leif to instruct the people of Greenland. Whether they sailed off course or purposely went in search of a new land, no one knows. But around the year 1000, Leif landed somewhere on the North American continent. Because of the good pastureland and the many wild grapes he found, Erikson called it Vinland. He and his companions spent the winter there; then they returned to Greenland.

ritories and voyages
of the Vikings

ONCE UPON A WORD

The way of life that monks and nuns follow is called *monasticism* (mo-NAS-ti-siz-uhm). Those who practice monasticism dedicate their whole lives to God in a monastery. These men and women make vows or promises to God. They give themselves to him by living and working together as a community. Each monastery follows a particular rule of life; for example, the Benedictines follow the Rule of Saint Benedict. The first monasteries had been founded centuries earlier. Yet they continued to develop and flourish as centers of culture, education, and faith. New communities, like the one at Cluny, were always being formed. As they multiplied and spread across Europe, their influence became a force in the world and within the Church. Today thousands of people still live consecrated lives in our world, some in monasteries!

"Hello. My name is Hugh and I am attending school here at the monastery. Well, actually I live here with the monks. When I am not studying or praying or doing my chores, I like to go into the studio where the monks are copying the Gospels by hand. That's how books are made. When I was told I could help the monks with 'illumination,' I thought I'd be holding a candle up to help them see what they were writing. It turns out that *illumination* is really a form of art. I guess the artist is 'lighting up' the story that the Gospel is telling. The monk-artists paint fancy first letters of each chapter with bright colors and pure gold. They also create paintings that look like a window right into the Gospel story. I wish that someday everyone will have an illuminated book, and I hope I'll get to make one!"

I Witness

The Holy Roman Empire

The event that most affected the Church was the revival of the Holy Roman Empire. After Charlemagne's death, the empire had become fragmented and weak. That changed in 962. Pope John XII crowned a German as Holy Roman Emperor Otto I (912–973). Seven years earlier, Otto had successfully stopped the march of the Magyars into Europe.

On the surface, it looked as though the pope and the emperor were working together. Underneath, however, the two men were very distrustful of each other. By making Otto the emperor, the pope gave him authority over the land that had belonged to the church centuries before, the Papal States. As soon as Otto left Rome, Pope John regretted the decision. And he sought the help of a neighboring king.

The emperor was furious. When he returned, he deposed Pope John XII and replaced him with a man who wasn't even a priest! This layman was consecrated as Pope Leo VIII. Of course, the emperor did not have legitimate authority to oust a pope. The result was that there were two popes at the same time. Eventually, Pope John XII died of a stroke while in exile. This ended a potential battle over who was really the pope.

Despite constant power struggles, renewing the emperor's position was beneficial; it did unify many lands. That unity made it easier to maintain strength, security, and stability.

Otto I   John XII

More than the Facts

In 964, a Persian astronomer composed a study called *The Book of Fixed Stars*. His name was Abd al-Rahman al-Sufi. Al-Sufi based his study on Ptolemy's second-century work, *The Almagest*, which was about the movement of stars and planets. *The Book of Fixed Stars* included all that was known about the various constellations at that time. It was finely illustrated and included the first known description of the Andromeda galaxy. Copies of this book are preserved today in scientific libraries.

The Book of Fixed Stars

Daily Life in the 10th Century

Most people in the tenth century lived their whole lives within a few miles' radius. Their days were full of hard work, insufficient food, poverty, illness, and illiteracy. Children were expected to contribute to supporting their families; they rarely had time for play. Nonetheless, many people found strength and inspiration in their faith. Common hardships were offset by the joy and satisfaction of growing up in and raising good Christian families.

Saint Wenceslaus

Wenceslaus or Vaclav I (around 907–935) became the ruling duke of Bohemia (now the Czech Republic) when he was only thirteen. Though his mother remained a pagan, Wenceslaus was a fervent Catholic who cared for his poorest subjects. Early biographers say he would not condemn any criminal to death; he preferred to encourage all to repent. After several years, rulers of neighboring kingdoms forced Wenceslaus to pay a large sum of money in exchange for protection against the invading Magyars. This loss of power angered his brother Boleslav so much that he had Wenceslaus murdered. Because of his goodness and piety, Wenceslaus was proclaimed a saint and legend calls him "king." You may be familiar with the Christmas carol "Good King Wenceslaus," which tells his story.

SNAPSHOT

On the Record

"Top of Form
O noble Rome, queen of the world and
of all the most important cities,
rose-colored with the blood of
martyrs,
lily-white with purity of virgins;
We greet you for everyone;
We bless you, Hail for all time!"

—Anonymous pilgrim hymn (10th century)

LATEST & GREATEST

Fireworks first appeared in China around the year 960. A man named Li Tian is considered the "father of the firecracker." It was such a popular invention that people offered sacrifices to him every April. Fireworks were usually bought from market vendors. The first fireworks were made of bamboo sticks filled with gunpowder.

Christianity in Russia

Whole new peoples were entering the Church. In 966 Mieszko I of Poland converted to faith in Christ. This began the eventual conversion of Poland. Vladimir I (956–1015) was grand duke of Kiev and all of Russia. With his baptism in 988, the Russian people were likewise encouraged to accept the faith. No one knows for certain, but it is believed that Christian teachings were secretly being circulated in Russia prior to Vladimir's baptism.

Although he was a grandson of Saint Olga, Vladimir had been raised as a pagan. He first came into contact with Christianity during a military campaign in Crimea. While there he attended the beautiful liturgies of the Eastern churches. Vladimir also heard of the beautiful sister of Emperor Basil II of Constantinople and asked to marry her. The emperor said it would only be possible if he were a Christian. Vladimir was now familiar with Christian teachings and requested baptism. When he returned to Kiev, Vladimir removed all the pagan shrines from the city. He also dedicated himself to establishing the church and educating his people. He built many monasteries and churches, including the grand Cathedral Church of St. Mary Ever-Virgin in 989. Then, seven years later, he built the Church of the Transfiguration in Kiev.

Because of his conversion and efforts to develop the Church in the East, Vladimir was given an exceptional title. He is referred to as "Equal to the Apostles" by the Russian Orthodox and other Eastern churches. This title is shared by great missionaries and promoters of the faith, such as Saint Mary Magdalene, Constantine the Great, and Saints Cyril and Methodius.

Vladimir & Anna

ACTIVITY

Make a map and label all the places mentioned in this chapter. Do you know anything about what was happening in areas not mentioned?

Prayer

Dear Lord, I am thankful to know that you keep watch over all of us. So many things happen every day throughout the world. We cannot know about all of them; we cannot be everywhere to help everyone, but you can. Show me how to accompany you with my prayers.
Amen.

The Bigger Picture

Power struggles have been simmering between church and government, as well as within the Church itself. By the end of this century, the disputes are about to boil over. Within a few decades the Church will divide, splintering Christianity. In both the East and the West, the Church will be less able to defend itself against conquests and violent invasions. Early questions about what Christians believe have largely been settled. Now, as the power of worldly rulers grows, the focus will shift. Both the Church and emerging nations will attempt to expand their power.

Great monasteries and religious orders will rise, fall into decline, and rise again. Many will appeal to the roots of religious life in order to renew the discipline and charisms that have decayed. Europe, as we think of it, is a long way off. Countries such as France, Germany, Spain, and Italy are still collections of small, often warring, kingdoms. Many will soon take up arms and fight for what they consider to be great and important causes. In a world of knights and vassals, true honor, courage, and loyalty will be highly valued—but rare.

Chapter 11

1002—Leif Ericsson leads a Viking expedition down the coast of North America.

AD 1012

AD 1024

1025—Avicenna of Persia finishes writing the five volume *Canon of Medicine*. It is used until the seventeenth century.

1028—Canute conquers Norway; his son becomes king of Norway.

1031—Chinese scholar Shen Kuo is born. In 1088 he writes *Mengxi Bitan* and becomes the first person to describe the concept of the magnetic needle compass.

AD 1036

AD 1048

AD 1060

1061—The Muslim Almoravid dynasty is founded in North Africa and later conquers Spain.

1067—Work begins on building the Tower of London.

AD 1072

AD 1084

AD 1096

1098—Saint Robert of Molesme founds the first Cistercian monastery at Cîteaux, France.

1099—Crusaders capture Jerusalem. Godfrey of Bouillon is elected ruler of the newly liberated Jerusalem.

East and West

The Great Schism

Pope Gregory and King Henry Disagree

Saints of the Century

Saint Margaret of Scotland

Saint Anselm

Saint Bruno

The First Crusade

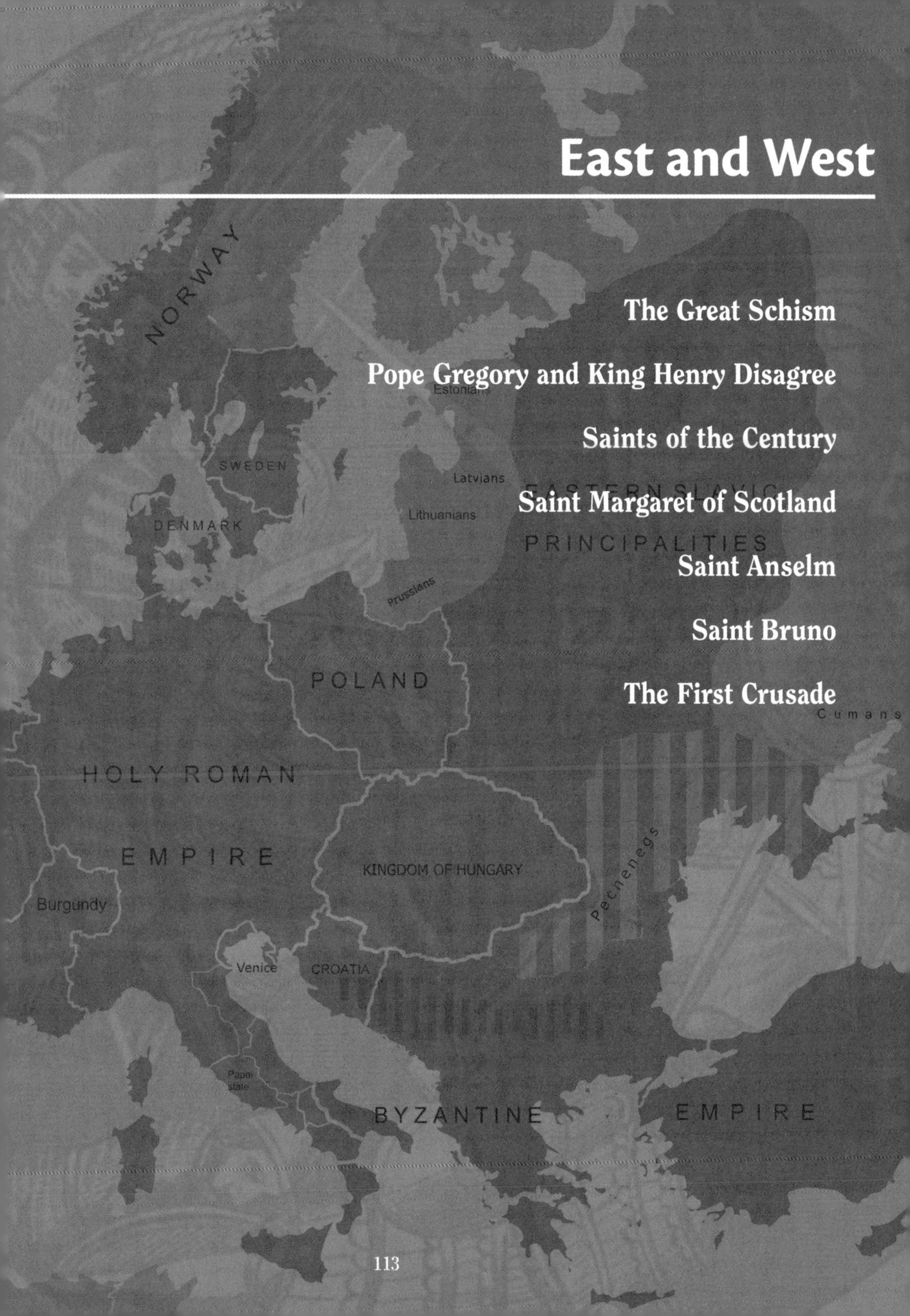
NORWAY
SWEDEN
DENMARK
Estonians
Latvians
Lithuanians
Prussians
EASTERN SLAVIC PRINCIPALITIES
POLAND
Cumans
HOLY ROMAN EMPIRE
KINGDOM OF HUNGARY
Pechenegs
Burgundy
Venice
CROATIA
Papal state
BYZANTINE EMPIRE

At the outset of the eleventh century, we hear again of the Vikings. Many of their disbanded armies had settled in northern and eastern England after the invasions. Mixing in with the local people, their families had grown numerous.

Ethelred II was the king of England. He feared the descendants of the Danish Vikings and thought they would attempt a takeover of his kingdom. Ethelred wanted to restore the entire land to English rule. So in 1002 he ordered a massacre of all the Vikings living in England.

To avenge the slaughter, Sweyn Forkbeard, king of Denmark, attacked England the following year with an army of Norsemen. He was victorious and by 1013 was proclaimed the king of England.

Between Sweyn's death in 1014 and the year 1042, the rule of England passed back and forth several times. One of the last Anglo-Saxon kings, Edward the Confessor, ruled England for more than twenty years. He focused much of his energy on building Westminster Abbey. Edward died in 1066. Because he had no children, a fight began over who would rule next. This led to an invasion the same year by William the Conqueror. With his victory at the Battle of Hastings, he became the first Norman king of England.

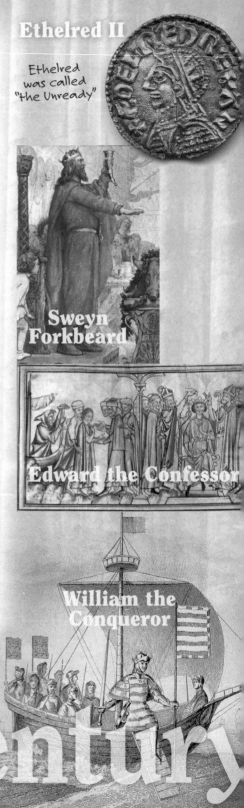

Ethelred II

Ethelred was called "the Unready"

Sweyn Forkbeard

Edward the Confessor

William the Conqueror

11th century

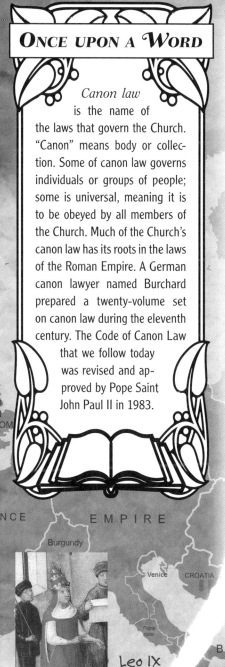

ONCE UPON A WORD

Canon law is the name of the laws that govern the Church. "Canon" means body or collection. Some of canon law governs individuals or groups of people; some is universal, meaning it is to be obeyed by all members of the Church. Much of the Church's canon law has its roots in the laws of the Roman Empire. A German canon lawyer named Burchard prepared a twenty-volume set on canon law during the eleventh century. The Code of Canon Law that we follow today was revised and approved by Pope Saint John Paul II in 1983.

Leo IX

Cerularius

The Great Schism

Meanwhile, the Church was facing a crisis, too. Since the time when Photius was patriarch of Constantinople, tension had grown between the Church in Rome and the Church in Constantinople. Now the patriarch of the East, Michael Cerularius, wanted to remove all Western Church influence by shutting down the Latin rite churches in Constantinople. Pope Leo IX sent three legates, or representatives, from Rome to negotiate with the patriarch. The situation worsened, however, and one of the representatives excommunicated Cerularius in July 1054. In response, Patriarch Cerularius excommunicated all three legates. The mutual excommunications were the final blow to the unity that the eastern and the western churches had enjoyed for centuries. This grievous split is known as the Great Schism. Both sides thought that the other was at fault; neither would reconcile with the other.

The fracture between the Church in the East and the Church in the West still exists today. Fortunately, Pope Paul VI and Patriarch Athenagoras I lifted the excommunications during Vatican Council II in 1965. More recently, meetings between the popes and the Eastern patriarchs have given fresh hope for eventual reconciliation.

Photius →

Pope Gregory and King Henry Disagree

Another important conflict over authority played out in the eleventh century. This conflict was over who had the power to choose bishops in the Church. Lay investiture—that is, the practice of kings bestowing ecclesial authority on a bishop—was a real problem. This may be an unfamiliar concept to us, but it is still important today. In order to practice our faith fully, the Church must be free to choose her own leaders. That is not always the case. To correct the practice, in 1075 Pope Gregory VII instituted a set of rules called the *Dictates of the Pope*. They were a major part of the Gregorian Reform. But Gregory's rules were not always followed, and two years later the problem came to a head.

The king of the Germans was Henry IV (1050–1106). He claimed for himself the authority to name bishops. He also seized the right to present them with the signs of their ecclesiastical office: their crosier and ring. Pope Gregory VII (1021–1085) immediately

On the Record

"My dearest son, if you want to give honor to the royal crown, I strongly advise you more than anything else to maintain the Catholic and apostolic faith diligently and carefully. May your example be seen by all whom God has put under your care. Then the clergy will clearly see that you are a man of true Christian belief. If you fail in this, you will certainly not be called a Christian or a son of the Church. Indeed, in the royal palace, after the faith itself, the Church holds second place....

However, dearest son, even now in our kingdom the Church is proclaimed as young and newly planted. For that reason she needs more prudent and trustworthy guardians. May the divine mercy bestowed on us undeservedly not be destroyed and annihilated through your idleness, laziness, or neglect."

—adapted from King Saint Stephen of Hungary (997–1038), *Admonitions* to his son, Emeric

excommunicated Henry in response. He then decided to travel to Germany to challenge the emperor about the matter. During the journey, Gregory paused to rest a while in the castle at Canossa, Italy. When the king heard of this, he went out to meet the pope. To restore his good standing with the Church, Henry presented himself as a humble penitent and asked for absolution. Once Pope Gregory was assured of Henry's sincerity, he granted the king forgiveness and absolved him from excommunication.

After this incident the Church and the king were reconciled for a time. Unfortunately, Henry went back on his word. Eventually he had Pope Gregory exiled. The pope died away from Rome in 1085. In our own time, civil rulers in nations like China continue to practice lay investiture. They appoint and install government-approved bishops against the wishes of the pope and Church leaders.

"Hello. I'm Gerta, and I'm a lucky girl. My parents and I live and work here in Canossa, the castle of Countess Matilda. Three days ago, the most amazing thing happened. While I was sweeping the inner steps, a beggar came to the gate. It was cold and snowy, but I noticed he had nothing on his feet. It turns out that the beggar was the King Henry IV! Can you believe it? He wanted Pope Gregory, who is staying here, to give him absolution for his sins. The pope refused to let him in until this morning. But just now the pope and the emperor came from chapel, where they were reconciled. Everyone hopes this will mean peace for the Church and the kingdom."

IWitness

Many great saints lived in the eleventh century.

Saint Margaret of Scotland

Because Saint Margaret (1046–1093) was a member of the royal house of Anglo-Saxons, she had to flee to Scotland when the Normans took over her country. There she married King Malcolm; together they had eight children. Margaret was a model Christian wife and mother. She exerted a loving and gentle influence on her husband and children. She also influenced the celebration of the liturgical seasons in the kingdom, founded monasteries, and promoted charitable works. Queen Margaret died at the age of forty-seven, shortly after receiving news that Malcolm and one of their sons had died in battle.

Margaret of Scotland

LATEST & GREATEST

Beginning in the eleventh century, the use of stained glass grew. It served as a way to light the inside of the great cathedrals and to catechize the faithful. This colored glass was created by a process of melting a combination of ash, sand, certain stones, and minerals. Colors came from the intensity of heat and the addition of different substances. Later, enamels and paints were burned onto the surface, to create depth and shadowing to the image depicted on the glass. After the glass cooled and was cut into shapes, it was mounted in place with strips of molten lead. Although stained glass was used in earlier ages, at this time church windows became illustrated "books" of instruction. The Augsburg Cathedral in Bavaria, Germany, still has in place the oldest stained glass windows in Europe; they date back to 1065. The windows depict the prophets Jonah, Daniel, Hosea, Moses, and David.

Saint Anselm

Saint Anselm (1033–1109) was archbishop of Canterbury from 1093 until his death. He defended the rights of the Church against Kings William II and Henry I, particularly with regard to the lay investiture problem. Anselm was the foremost theologian of his time. He is best known for his work on the existence of God. Saint Anselm is honored as a great mystic and theologian; he was also named a doctor of the Church. Anselm laid the groundwork for what would become the doctrine of Mary's Immaculate Conception.

SAINT ANSELME

Anselm

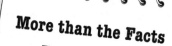

Bruno

Saint Bruno

Saint Bruno (1035–1101) was well educated and was appointed to serve at the cathedral of Rheims. After a few years, Bruno requested permission to retire with six companions as hermits. They founded the Carthusian order. They lived in the hills of Chartreuse above Grenoble in alpine France. Bruno was later called to Rome as a councilor to Pope Urban II. He refused to be appointed a bishop when the pope invited him. Bruno happily spent the rest of his life as a hermit.

More than the Facts

The very first novel ever was written in Japan by Lady Murasaki Shikibu. Completed around the year 1000, the book was entitled, *The Tale of Genji*. It tells the life and adventures of a prince and his companions.

Mystery of History

Eilmer, a monk of Malmesbury Abbey in England, may have been the first man to take flight. The historian William of Malmesbury wrote about it a hundred years later. It seems that Eilmer made a pair of wings and attempted to fly from a monastery roof. He landed hard, however, and broke both of his legs. They gave him trouble for the rest of his life. But there is a lot we don't know about this story. How did Eilmer construct wings? How far did he "fly"? Did he simply glide down a hillside or did he soar over buildings?

QVI ... VE E ABITO
GVIL ... MONACO

SNAPSHOT

Guido d'Arezzo

Guido d'Arezzo (around 995–1050) was a Benedictine monk in Arezzo, Italy. He wanted to make it easier for others to learn to sing the Church's chants. To accomplish this, Guido taught singers to "read" the music and not merely memorize it. He began by adding two lines to the staff, making four-line staffs (staves). He then named each of the six tones after the first syllable in each line of a hymn to Saint John: *ut, re*sonare, *mi*ra, *fa*muli, *so*lve, *la*bii. Eventually *ut* was replaced by *do*. One more tone was added, *ti*, before reaching the next higher *do*. *Do, re, mi, fa, so, la, ti, do*: this is the musical scale we use today, but in North America we usually refer to it with the letters C-D-E-F-G-A-B. Using Guido d'Arezzo's notes, composers could write down their music and have it sung more accurately by others. His method was so successful that Pope John XIX asked Guido to come to Rome and teach it. Not much is known of Guido's life after he returned to Arezzo. He is known as the father of musical notation.

Vt re mi fa sol la   la sol fa mi re ut

D · PELONI · P · AN · CIƆIƆCCCXX

The First Crusade

Despite the division between eastern and western Christians, the bishop of Rome received a call for help from the East. Much of the Holy Land had fallen into the hands of Muslims. It was extremely difficult for Christians to live there, or even to visit.

The pope responded to this call for help in 1095 at the Council of Clermont. Urban II called for Christian armies to go on a crusade; they were to defend believers in the East and liberate the holy places. Incentives were offered for those who went. They would be granted a plenary indulgence, which meant all punishment due for their sins would be remitted. Crusaders even believed that if they died in battle, they would be martyrs.

Armies assembled throughout Europe. Thousands of soldiers were led by nobles and princes. Together they defeated the Muslim armies and liberated the Holy Land. One of the leaders of the Crusade, Godfrey of Bouillon, was chosen to be the leader of Jerusalem. He refused to take the title of king. Instead he became the "Defender of the Holy Sepurchre."

When the Crusade first started, its goals were noble and just. The Holy Father made it clear that killing innocent people was forbidden. Unfortunately, some crusaders went beyond simply defending Christians in the East; they used the Crusade as an opportunity for violence and plunder. Serious immoral actions detracted from the noble purpose of the campaigns and reflected badly on all crusaders. The purpose of the Crusades had been to assist the Church of the East against the Muslim persecution. But soon Latin rite bishops were establishing themselves in Eastern dioceses. They wanted to minister to Latin rite Catholics who had traveled there. Eastern churches considered this unwelcome Western aggression, and new tensions developed.

Godfrey of Bouillon

ACTIVITY

Investigate how cathedrals were built and . . .

1. try building a model cathedral out of building blocks or other materials;

2. as a class project, design a cathedral for today. Have each class member work on a different aspect, for example, floor plans, windows, statuary, masonry, design of grounds, choosing a local site, furnishings, tapestries and/or banners;

3. pay a visit to the cathedral of your home diocese. Make notes about its main features.

Prayer

My God, I see that the Church can make use of whatever natural gifts each of us has. Help me recognize what my gifts and talents are. May I use them to serve you and your Church. Protect me from jealousy of others. Each of us is important; together our abilities express how blessings are given to be shared.
Amen.

The Bigger Picture

Christian Europe has again grown strong enough to challenge Muslim hold in the Holy Land. The age of the Crusades will begin in earnest. It will be a time of suffering and complex choices, but also an age of Christian idealism and true holiness. Many saints will appear in the coming century, including Saint Bernard, Saint Hildegard, and Saint Thomas à Becket. Each will influence the events of their day in a way that will also shape the future.

The next century will show us how the lives and works of individuals can influence and enhance powerful institutions and movements. History is really the story of the people, the individuals of each century. The truly memorable individuals of any period are those whose lives stand out against the events of the time. Sometimes people are remembered for the part they played in evil events. As Christians, we repent for any wrongs we have committed. We rejoice in the many persons who lived virtuous, useful, and often heroic lives.

Chapter 12

AD 1110

AD 1120   1119—Hugues de Payens founds the Order of Knights Templar.

AD 1130   1128—Portugal wins independence from Spain.

AD 1140

AD 1150

   1154—Adrian IV (Nicholas Breakspear), the only Englishman to become pope, begins his reign.

AD 1160

   1161—Explosives are first used in China at the battle of Ts'ai-shih.

AD 1170

   1182—Philip II banishes Jews from France.

AD 1180   1182—Maronite Christians in Lebanon reaffirm their union with the Church of Rome.

   1187–Saladin recaptures Jerusalem for Muslim rule.

   1190—Barbarossa dies on the way to Palestine;
AD 1190   Henry VI becomes the new Holy Roman emperor in 1191.

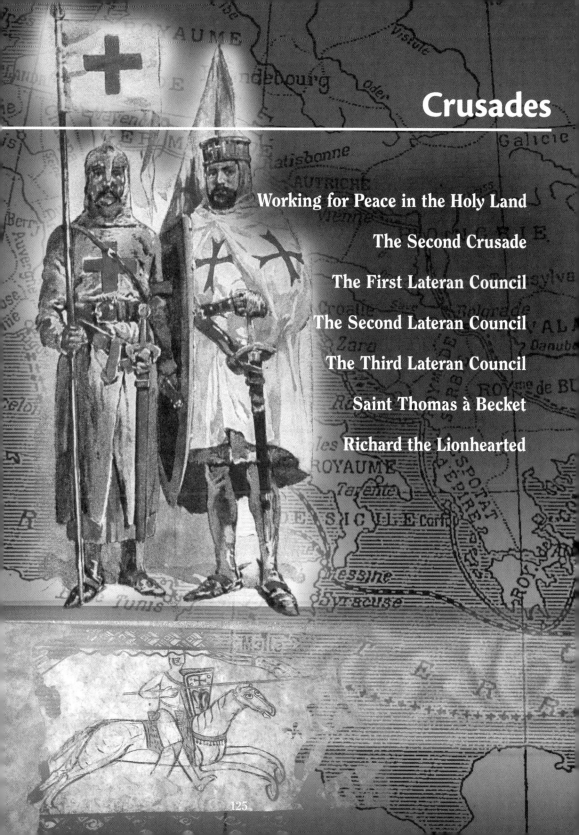

Crusades

During the twelfth century, Crusades continue to dominate the Church history landscape. Crusaders were viewed by the Church as military pilgrims. As a result, knighthood became more strongly connected to the faith. Men hoping to become knights were often required to fast, confess their sins, and dedicate their weapons to the Church and to God. The new order imposed by the crusaders in the East opened up trade routes that had been closed since the time of ancient Rome. This made the West more prosperous than it had been in quite some time. Muslims, however, were quietly rebuilding their armies. They were making plans to reconquer the territory they had lost.

a knight Templar

12th century

Working for Peace in the Holy Land

The conquest of the Holy Land in the First Crusade had led to the *Truce of God*. This was a sacred agreement intended to guarantee the safety of Christians who traveled to the Holy Land. It was an extension of what had been known as the *Peace of God*, which began before the tenth century. These pacts tried to limit violence and ensure the safety of clergy, farmers, merchants, women, and children during frequent feudal wars. The pact also dictated the times and places where fighting was permitted. For example, the common area in front of the church was to be respected. Sundays and holy days were to be peaceful; this eventually expanded to include the entire seasons of Advent and Lent, and then a number of other significant days. These efforts to establish the peace that Christ himself promised were somewhat effective in Europe. They did not, however, succeed in the face of warfare with forces not under the Church's jurisdiction.

Emperor Conrad III

King Louis VII

The Second Crusade

By 1147 Muslim forces had reclaimed the county of Edessa in present-day Turkey; it was an important stopping point on the route to the Holy Land. A second crusade was called by Pope Eugene III. Saint Bernard, the abbot of Clairvaux, was asked to preach the need for this new campaign. Bernard did so, but he also insisted that Christian soldiers respect Orthodox Christians and not pillage their properties or their churches. Bernard also warned the crusaders against anti-Semitism, or committing acts of hatred toward the Jewish people they encountered. These principles were not always followed. The Second Crusade was led by King Louis VII of France and Emperor Conrad III of Germany. The armies did not cooperate with one another, however. Ironically, the emperor of Constantinople was afraid the crusaders might sack his city, so he made an alliance with the Muslim forces for protection.

"Godfrey is my name. I'm going to be a knight when I grow up. Not just a fighting knight, but one like my uncle Stephen. He is a Knight Templar in Jerusalem. The real name of his order is *The Poor Fellow-Soldiers of Christ and of the Temple of Solomon*. Uncle Stephen is a soldier-monk. Together with his brothers, he is protecting the places made holy by the life of Christ and the pilgrims who come to visit them. I think my uncle is a real hero."

I Witness

CALISTVS·II·PP·GALVS·

this is Pope Callistus II

HENRI V.

this is Henry V

The First Lateran Council

Meanwhile, the Church was fighting a different type of battle. In September 1122 the Holy Roman Emperor Henry V gave up his claim to the right of naming bishops and investing them with Church power (lay investiture). Now the choice and investiture of bishops would be done within each diocese. This conclusion was known as the Concordat, or agreement, of Worms (pronounced VERMS); it was so named for the German city that hosted the meeting.

In 1123 the First Lateran Council was called in Rome, where hundreds of participants confirmed what the concordat had stated. This council marked the beginning of the separation of Church and state. An emperor could no longer claim a divine right to name the pope or bishops. The council also made decrees against simony, that is, the buying of positions within the Church; forgery of Church documents; and theft of Church money or property. It also required that Roman Catholic priests remain unmarried celibates from then on.

LATEST & GREATEST

The mariner's compass was invented in China during the Song dynasty. It was the first time a magnetic needle was used for navigation. While Shen Kuo first described the concept of the compass in 1088, the earliest record of its use is in a book written in 1119 by Zhu Yu. It did not take long for sailors to find it useful in the Arabian sea. From there, the compass spread to European sailing vessels as well.

The Second Lateran Council

Pope Innocent II called the Second Lateran Council in 1139. This council had the specific task of officially condemning the teaching of Arnold of Brescia (around 1090–1155). Arnold was a monk who preached against the wealth of the Church, and especially the wealth of the clergy. While he may well have had good reason for concern, Arnold took things too far. He told laypeople that they should take upon themselves the authority of the clergy, including giving the sacraments to one another.

The Third Lateran Council

Pope Alexander III called the Third Lateran Council in 1179. The council was again called to address moral practices and to condemn two more heretical groups: the Albigenses and Waldenses. They shared a common distrust of anything material. Albigensians believed in a god of good (spiritual world) and a god of evil (material world). Waldensians preached that all wealth was wrong; they ended up separating themselves from the sacramental life of the Church. In addition, the council also established that a pope's election must require two-thirds of the bishops present to vote for him.

INNOCENTIVS·II·PP·ROMANVS

More than the Facts

Cymbals were introduced to Europe as a percussion instrument in the twelfth century. They were originally from Turkey, Tibet, and India. Cymbals have been around for thousands of years. They were used to frighten enemy armies, worship gods, signal danger, beg for money, and even to call honeybees back to their hives!

Saint Thomas à Becket

Henry II

Thomas

In England King Henry II was trying to strengthen his own power. One way he thought of accomplishing this was to appoint his friend and chancellor, Thomas à Becket (1118–1170), as the archbishop of Canterbury. This would make the leading bishop in England a personal friend of the king.

The results, however, were not what King Henry had expected. Instead of doing whatever the king wanted him to do as archbishop, Thomas defended the rights of the Church. Eventually, the king was so angry at him that Thomas had to escape to France and hide in a monastery. In 1170, the two were reconciled and Thomas returned to Canterbury; once again he took up his duties as archbishop. The king, however, grew agitated by Thomas' refusal to conform to

On the Record

Saint Thomas à Becket, archbishop of Canterbury, to King Henry II of England, from whom the archbishop had fled (1166):

"If you value your soul, my lord, cease depriving the Church of her rights. Keep in mind the promise you made to protect the Church's liberty. You laid this promise on the altar at Westminster when you were consecrated and anointed king by my predecessor. Return, then, to the Church of Canterbury . . . the rank it held during the time of our predecessors. Return too all the Church's possessions, towns, castles, and farms, as well as whatever else was violently taken either from myself or from anyone dependent on me, laymen or clerics. And, if it pleases you, let us return freely and in peace with all liberty to our see [diocese]. May we perform the duties of our office as we should. We are ready to serve you faithfully with all our strength as our dearest lord and king, however we are able. We intend to do this while protecting the honor of God and of the Roman Church, and our own duty."

his expectations. Then he made a fatal mistake. Without thinking of the consequences, King Henry complained to some of his knights, saying: "Will no one rid me of this troublesome priest?" Taking these words as a command, four knights immediately rode off to Canterbury. When they arrived they demanded to see the archbishop. The servants tried to bar the door, but Thomas told them that no one should be kept out of God's house. The knights then rushed in and killed the archbishop right near the altar. When the news reached King Henry, he deeply regretted what had been done in his name. He had a shrine set up in Canterbury Cathedral to honor Thomas à Becket. He even went there himself to perform public acts of penance. Thomas was declared a martyr and canonized in 1173.

ONCE UPON A WORD

The term *Gothic* is often used to describe dark and frightening things. It originally referred to the Germanic people called Goths. In the twelfth century their name was given to a new style of architecture. Gothic cathedrals were large and strong in appearance, with great arches. They often had supports along the sides called "flying buttresses," which look like the wings of a bird at rest.

Mystery of History

How does the Leaning Tower of Pisa, begun in 1173, keep from falling down? This famous 185-foot bell tower began to lean when the second floor was being built. It took 344 years to complete, because construction of the tower was interrupted by wars. First it leaned north. The builders made the columns taller on that side and hung the heavier bells on the south side. Then it began to sink to the south. The problem is that the soil is very wet beneath it. The area had been a lagoon centuries ago.

Currently the tower is leaning seventeen feet to the south of its axis. It was restored between 1989 and 2000. In 2008, engineers examining the tower reported that it had stopped moving. Despite its precarious tilt and the predictions of physicists throughout history, the Tower of Pisa continues to defy gravity.

Richard the Lionhearted

The son of Henry II was known as Richard the Lionhearted. Richard, who reigned from 1189 to 1199, considered it his duty to go on crusade. He heard that the Muslim general, Saladin, had captured Jerusalem. So he joined Frederick Barbarossa, the Roman emperor and king of Germany (1122–1190), and Philip II of France to lead the Third Crusade. After defeating Saladin at Acre and Jaffa, Richard was captured on the way home from the Crusade. During his absence, his younger brother John attempted to steal the throne from him. Their mother, Eleanor of Aquitane, intervened; she forced John to pledge his loyalty to Richard. In 1194 Richard was ransomed and returned to power in England. John wisely sought refuge in France. Unfortunately, King Richard died a few years later, during a battle in France in 1199. John, the jealous younger brother, eventually became one of the worst kings in England's history.

SNAPSHOT

Saint Hildegard of Bingen

Saint Hildegard of Bingen (1098–1179) was one of the most learned and influential women of her time. As a child she was always sick. it was feared she would not be able to accomplish much. When she was eight her parents put her in the care of an old nun named Jutta. Hildegard learned to read and even to chant the Liturgy of the Hours. This consists of psalms and prayers recited daily at the time by priests, monks, and nuns. Eventually, others joined Jutta, and they formed a Benedictine monastery in her native Germany. Hildegard became the superior in 1136 when Jutta died.

Over the years Hildegard wrote books about everything from medical practices to natural history and biblical commentaries. She even created a new alphabet. Hildegard also wrote a lot of letters to important people of her day. She is best known for her book of visions called *Scivias* (SKI-vee-ahs), or "ways of light."

Hildegard also had a deeply mystical prayer life. From the time she was three years old, she often saw mysterious things about God and the history of salvation. These visions frightened her because no one else could see them. Hildegard's bishop and the pope, Eugene III, studied her mystical experiences for many years. Eventually, Hildegard's visions were approved; they were officially recognized as coming to her from God. She was even asked to write them down for others.

Because of her wisdom and prayerfulness, many people sought Hildegard's advice. She also traveled around Germany to visit the other monasteries she had founded.

When Hildegard died she was venerated as a saint. She was not officially canonized until 2012 by Pope Benedict XVI. He also declared Hildegard a doctor of the Church. She is only the fourth woman in the history of the Church to receive that title. Saint Hildegard of Bingen's feast day is September 17.

ACTIVITY

Look on the map to find the Temple Mount where the Knights Templar had their headquarters in Jerusalem. Can you calculate how many miles the knights and crusaders had to travel from their homes in Europe to the Holy Land? How long do you think it took them to reach there?

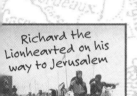

Richard the Lionhearted on his way to Jerusalem

Prayer

My Lord, this century seems full of energy and activity, but not all of it seems good. Today we think that some of the campaigns and crusades that kings and popes carried out were bad ideas. But only you can understand and judge people's thoughts and intentions. Perhaps in the future others will think that the choices we are making now are wrong or mistaken. Lord, help me to concentrate on the good that I can do. May my "crusade" be truly noble and just. May what I do always help others. Amen.

The Bigger Picture

The century witnessed much activity. After many efforts at both war and peace, people returned to their homes with a yearning for normality and peace. Even in parts of the world far from the center of Christianity, people were on the move. They hoped to settle where they could build good and peaceful lives.

Peoples moved and mixed in times of famine and war. They searched for better living conditions for themselves and their families. By the end of this century the colonization of Polynesian islands by Southeast Asians was nearly complete. People discovered and settled in a vast area stretching from New Zealand north to Hawaii and east to Rapa Nui (Easter Island). By the middle of the twelfth century, the Mexican Toltec Empire had come to an end. Many of its people joined the Mayans on the Yucatán Peninsula.

Change and movement were coming within the Church as well. By the dawn of the thirteenth century, Christians were weary of war and corruption. They were also starving for real spiritual nourishment. In the coming century, God would raise up amazing men like Saint Francis and Saint Dominic. They would rebuild the Church and provide new ways to satisfy people's longing for God.

Chapter 13

1202—Leonardo Fibonacci promotes the use of Arabic numerals in Europe.

AD 1210

1211—Genghis Khan invades China.

1215—English barons force King John to sign the Magna Carta, an agreement to honor their rights.

AD 1220

AD 1230

1232—Mongols and Chinese first use rockets in war. The Chinese are defeated.

AD 1240

AD 1250

AD 1260

AD 1270

1274—The Synod of Lyons recommends that papal elections remain secret to avoid corruption.

1275–1292—Marco Polo serves Kublai Khan.

AD 1280

1280—Albert the Great, a Dominican philosopher, dies.

1289—John of Montecorvino is named the first archbishop of Peking (now Beijing)

AD 1290

Friars on the Front Lines

Effects of the Crusades

Saint Francis of Assisi
and His Followers

Saint Dominic and His Followers

The Fourth Lateran Council
(and the Eucharist)

The Miracle of Bolsena
and the Feast of Corpus Christi

The Crusades Continue

An unfortunate event happened at the start of the thirteenth century. The Fourth Crusade turned its attention not to the Muslims, but to the Christian city of Constantinople. Crusaders from Venice invaded and sacked Constantinople in early 1204. Adding insult to injury, the Venetians stole the relic of Saint Mark from the Orthodox Church and brought it back to Venice. The crusaders also set up a western empire in Constantinople. They installed a Latin rite, or Roman Catholic, patriarch. This embittered the Orthodox toward Rome.

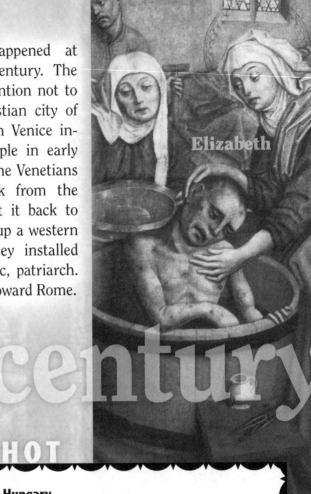

Elizabeth

13th century

SNAPSHOT

Saint Elizabeth of Hungary

Saint Elizabeth of Hungary (1207–1231) was born a princess. It was customary back then for royalty to promise their children in marriage to other royal families. At age four Elizabeth went to Thuringia, Germany, to be brought up with Hermann; he was the boy who was to be her future husband. Hermann soon died, however. Elizabeth was then promised to Hermann's brother, Ludwig. Their marriage began in 1221 and was very happy. They became the parents of three children. Elizabeth was a prayerful young woman. She especially delighted in helping the poor.

Then Ludwig died in 1227 while on a crusade. Filled with grief, Elizabeth felt sure her life, too, was over. It is uncertain whether she was sent away from the castle by jealous relatives or whether she left willingly. Soon, however, she was out on her own. Her children were taken away to live with her deceased husband's family. Elizabeth was given back her dowry of two thousand marks. She immediately gave a fourth of it to the poor and became a Third Order Franciscan. She then built a hospital in Marburg where she cared for the most seriously ill. Soon her own strength was consumed, and she died at the age of twenty-four. Elizabeth was proclaimed a saint by Pope Gregory IX in 1235. Today many hospitals and healthcare facilities around the world bear her name.

Effects of the Crusades

Although the Crusades were meant to bring glory to the name of God and peace to the Christian people, they also caused much suffering. As with any war, numbers of soldiers who went on crusades never returned. They left families behind with little hope of support. The Crusades did open up trade routes to the East, which brought increasing wealth to merchants and the ruling classes. However, discontent grew between the rich and the poor.

Heresies like Catharism and Waldensianism continued to appear. They taught that is was necessary to live in extreme poverty, the way the early Christians did. While the people believing these heresies were wrongheaded, they were not necessarily wronghearted. The Church had become absorbed with worldly power and wealth. In some instances, Church leaders were even immoral and corrupt. The Church was not always providing a clear example of Christian virtue; it was not giving a convincing witness to the Gospel of Jesus Christ.

Mystery of History

Did children actually go on a crusade in 1212?

Thousands of "children" left France to join a Children's Crusade. Some historians think these crusaders were legally still "boys" or unmarried young men. Others believe that many were not older than their leader, a twelve-year-old boy named Stephen. All agree that boys of varied ages did come together from France and Germany with the intention of going on crusade. Inspired by the adults of their times, they made banners and traveled to Italy, but were either turned back or shipwrecked. None of them made it to the Holy Land. What little historical evidence exists suggests that the boys were not trained soldiers. It seems that most were captured and sold into slavery.

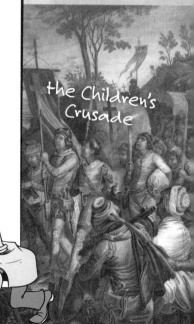

the Children's Crusade

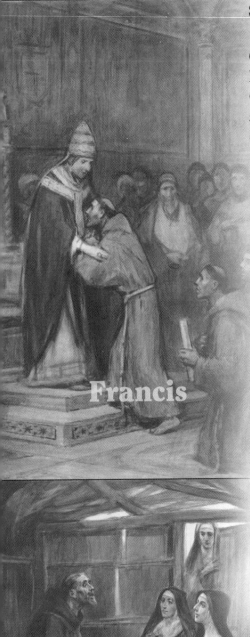

Francis

Clare

Saint Francis of Assisi and His Followers

In the midst of this troubling situation, God inspired a young man in Assisi, Italy. He would become a striking example of true Christian poverty. Francis (1181–1226), the son of a wealthy cloth merchant, was typical of many young people. He tried living a carefree life; he tried being a soldier; he even tried the life of a merchant. In all his efforts, he remained dissatisfied.

One day he heard the voice of God say: "Francis, repair my church." At first Francis thought God wanted him to rebuild a nearby chapel. In time he realized he was being called to help renew the life of God's people.

Francis gathered companions to himself. They did not condemn wealth, but they personally renounced the riches of the world. Together they dedicated their energies to works of charity and to preaching the Gospel. Instead of condemning the faults of other Christians, these new Franciscans led others to holiness by their own example.

Among those who followed Saint Francis were a rich young woman of Assisi named Clare (1193–1253), a monk named Anthony of Padua (1195–1231), and a duchess named Elizabeth of Hungary (1207–1231). These three, along with many others, learned from Saint Francis to value the poverty of spirit Christ had taught in the Beatitudes. They, too, became saints.

Saint Dominic and His Followers

Around this same time another man followed the Lord's inspiration to found a new religious community. This man was Saint Dominic (1170–1221). He began the Order of Preachers, known today as the Dominicans. As the title of his order suggests, Dominic wanted to train men and women to preach the Gospel and the teachings of the Church. Dominic did this partly to prevent the faithful from being led astray by false teachings. But he also wanted to instruct people to strengthen their understanding of and commitment to the Christian faith. Among those who joined the Dominicans were the lawyer-priest Raymond of Penyafort (1175–1275); the philosopher Albert the Great (1206–1280); and perhaps the greatest theologian of all, Thomas Aquinas (1225–1274).

In giving themselves to Christ, Saint Francis and Saint Dominic gave the Church new pathways of holiness.

Dominic

oldest image of Saint Dominic by an unknown artist of the 14th century

On the Record

The greatest teacher of Scripture and theology in all of Church history was Saint Thomas Aquinas (1225–1274). Besides being a scholar, Thomas was a man of profound prayer. Near the end of his life, he was observed by several other monks to be in a deep state of prayer. They heard Christ on the crucifix say to Thomas: "You have written well of me; what reward can I give you?" Thomas humbly answered, "Nothing more than yourself, Lord." After this Thomas claimed he could no longer write. He laid aside his pen, saying, "There is nothing else I can do. Such secrets have been revealed to me that it seems all I have written until now is like a pile of straw."

—William of Tocco, *Ystoria sancti Thome de Aquino de Guillaume de Tocco* (1323)

The Fourth Lateran Council (and the Eucharist)

The thirteenth century could be called the Century of the Holy Eucharist. This is because of three unique events. The first of these was the Fourth Ecumenical Lateran Council (November 11–30, 1215); it defined *transubstantiation* (TRAN-suhb-STAN-shee-AY-shuhn). This very long word is how we describe what happens to the bread and wine at Mass. As Catholics, we believe that the bread and wine we offer to God are completely changed into the Body and Blood of Christ during the Eucharistic Prayer. While the bread and wine *appear* to be the same, their substance has changed. This is a mystery of our faith, and a great gift from God. It is something that the Church had always believed, even though it was not defined until this council. The Fourth Ecumenical Lateran Council also established the "Easter duty"; this requires Catholics to go to confession and receive the Holy Eucharist at least once a year.

ONCE UPON A WORD

The word *inquisition* means a questioning or investigation. From the thirteenth to the fifteenth centuries, the Church set up a tribunal or court called an inquisition. Its purpose was to identify, examine, and punish anyone who publicly opposed the Church and taught against the faith. These people were put on trial as heretics. Some had converted to the faith and then went back to their former beliefs. Those who were found guilty were turned over to the state for punishment. The most well known of these trials was the Spanish Inquisition.

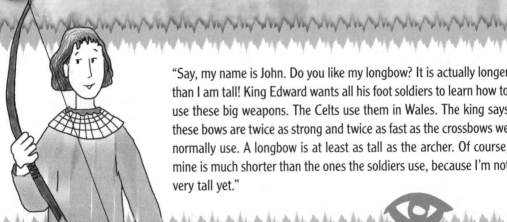

"Say, my name is John. Do you like my longbow? It is actually longer than I am tall! King Edward wants all his foot soldiers to learn how to use these big weapons. The Celts use them in Wales. The king says these bows are twice as strong and twice as fast as the crossbows we normally use. A longbow is at least as tall as the archer. Of course, mine is much shorter than the ones the soldiers use, because I'm not very tall yet."

I Witness

The Miracle of Bolsena

The Miracle of Bolsena and the Feast of Corpus Christi

The second event related to the Eucharist is called the Miracle of Bolsena. In 1263, a priest from the city of Prague stopped to celebrate Mass at the Church of St. Christina. He was a good priest but had some doubts about the real presence of Jesus in the Eucharist. As he was consecrating the bread, the Host began to bleed! The priest brought the Host and the blood-stained linen to Pope Urban IV, who was staying in the nearby city of Orvieto, Italy. The pope had the Host and linen enshrined at the cathedral.

Later Pope Urban IV created the Feast of Corpus Christi (Body of Christ). This is the third event related to the Eucharist. Corpus Christi was celebrated for the first time in 1264. The pope also asked Saint Thomas Aquinas to write beautiful hymns for this new celebration. We still sing them today: the *Adoro Te* (Godhead Here in Hiding, You I Do Adore) and the *Pange Lingua* (Sing, My Tongue).

More than the Facts

One of the oldest boys' choirs of Europe began in the thirteenth century. The church of St. Nicholas in Dresden, Germany, gathered a group of young boys to enhance the liturgy with their pure voices. Over the centuries the church was renamed Kreuzkirche or Church of the Holy Cross. A few hundred years later, during the Protestant Reformation, the church became a Lutheran parish. The boys' choir, Dresden Kreuzchor, has continued singing for church services and in concerts around the world even to the present day.

Louis IX

The Crusades Continue

Despite the deeply felt desire for peace, Christians continued their crusades. Some were successful in winning access to the holy places in Jerusalem; others were not. Throughout the fifth through the eighth Crusades it seemed like Christians were playing a game of chess with the Muslims. By the end of the thirteenth century, all the territory won by the crusaders had been recaptured by Muslim forces.

What then was gained by the many years of Crusades? A sense of Christian idealism and a heroic challenge were stirred up. In fact, even saints went on crusade. Most notable in this century was Saint Louis IX of France. He went on the Seventh Crusade in 1248, but lost the majority of his army before returning home. He set out again on the Eighth Crusade, but died of dysentery in 1270 in the Crusader camp at Tunis in North Africa.

The Crusades provided insight into the culture of the East. They also helped establish certain important trade routes. However, the cost was great. The violence of war and the destruction done to Constantinople, as well as the takeover of power of the East by the West, further damaged relations between the churches. At the Council of Lyons, France (1274), the two churches united, but only temporarily. The division between them had become too deep.

LATEST & GREATEST

A note about eyeglasses was found in Venice in 1286. In it the glasses are called "little discs for the eyes." Glasses at this time were either a single disc of glass held in front of the eye or a double set balanced on the nose. No one knows for certain who first invented eyeglasses; variations were mentioned as far back as the Greeks. In his writings, the English Franciscan Roger Bacon (1220–1292) states that letters can be seen more clearly through a glass sphere.

ACTIVITY

Investigate what makes a particular year a holy year. When was the last holy year? Which year will be the next one? Or research a Church solemnity or feast. When and why do we celebrate Christ the King, the Assumption of Mary, or the Immaculate Conception? How were these special days established?

Prayer

Dear Jesus, make me brave and determined like the heroes of the thirteenth century. Give me a deep love for the Eucharist and a strong faith in the real presence of your Body and Blood. Teach me to follow your inspirations. Help me to be open to your will and always ready to share your teachings with others. Amen.

The Bigger Picture

With the Crusades, the people of the Medieval Christian world made a great quest for peace. At the time there must have been hopes that war would never again draw armies so far away from their homelands. Yet wars would continue through all the centuries to come. In the fourteenth century, for example, we will see the beginning of the great Hundred Years' War between France and Britain.

The thirteenth century witnessed the Church taking up a "war" against heresy with the Inquisition. It started at the Council of Toulouse in France in 1229. The first Inquisition was set up as a court to question those teaching the Cathar heresy. Within about thirty years, however, the questioners began to use threats and torture to force people to confess their false beliefs.

As you can imagine, these extreme methods not only brought great suffering to heretics; they also hurt the Church. In her efforts to defend truth, the Church lost sight of the fact that acceptance of the truth cannot be forced. Over the next few centuries the Church learned that truth must always be offered as an invitation. She also came to realize the importance of remaining above the ways of worldly power in order to protect the message of salvation that Jesus Christ entrusted to her.

Fortunately, however, a great spirit of prayer prevailed among the faithful. New religious movements, like those begun by Saint Francis and Saint Dominic, rebuilt the Church's spiritual strength. It is important to note that just before the fourteenth century dawned, the Church celebrated the first holy year on record. It opened on February 22, 1300.

Chapter 14

AD 1310

1305—The Scottish rebel and hero William Wallace is captured and executed by the English.

1306—Robert the Bruce is crowned King of Scotland. Within seven years, the English are defeated and Scotland gains independence.

AD 1310

1310–1320—Dante Alighieri writes *The Divine Comedy*.

AD 1320

1325—Aztecs arrive in Tenochtitlán (Mexico City).

AD 1330

1337–1453—The Hundred Years' War takes place between France and England.

AD 1340

1347—The Black Death plague spreads through Europe.

AD 1350

AD 1360

AD 1370

1387—Lithuanians convert to Christianity.

AD 1380

1387—Geoffrey Chaucer writes *The Canterbury Tales*.

1390—The shroud of Jesus (now known as the Shroud of Turin) is discovered in Lirey, France.

AD 1390

1392—The Yi Dynasty in Korea begins. It will endure until 1910.

Return to Rome

Divisions often teach us the value of unity. This is true among individuals and within families. It is also true within the Church. Several big divisions occurred during the fourteenth century. One of these involved a whole army of individuals. Another had to do with the papacy. The third was the rise of still more heresies.

a craftsman of the silk guild

14th century

"Welcome to beautiful Florence, Italy. I'm Gina, and my family belongs to the Silk Guild. Mama teaches the newest weaving techniques to the craftsmen. Papa imports the delicate little silkworms—actually their eggs and cocoons—from the Eastern merchants. I'm helping him plant mulberry trees, the favorite food of silkworms. If the trees can grow here, we'll be able to farm our own silkworms, too. Imagine: I could be head of the Silk Guild some day!"

I Witness

More than the Facts

In 1347 a highly contagious plague appeared in Europe and caused widespread death. It was called the Black Death. One-third of the population of most countries, and nearly half of the English, died within five years. This disease, the bubonic plague, was carried by fleas on the rats that stowed away on trading ships from the Orient. Before it reached Europe, the illness had already wiped out large numbers of people throughout all the countries on the trade route known as the Silk Road.

Hugues de Payens
co-founder and
first Grand
Master of the
Knights Templar

King Philip the
Fair of France

The Knights Templar

Many noblemen had joined the Crusades with the intention of freeing the Holy Land from the Muslims. As time went on, a good number of crusaders saw a new way of life emerge from this experience. They joined together to form brotherhoods of soldier-monks. The Church encouraged this because of the good intention these men had. They were totally dedicated to God's service.

One of these brotherhoods was the Knights Templar. They were heroic in battle but lived as monks at home. In gratitude for their service, the Knights Templar were given many properties. Other people became jealous of the knights' wealth and influence and accused them of various crimes, including heresy.

In 1310, Pope Clement V called a council to settle the controversy. These soldier-monks had served for many years in the Crusades. They were the first-line men who had freed the Holy Land and continued to defend it.

When King Philip the Fair of France began thinking of where to get money to finance a new crusade, he set his sights on the wealth of the Templars. He could not simply take it, because the Templars were responsible only to the Church. So instead, he made a deceitful plan. While young Knights Templar were fighting in foreign lands, King Philip accused them of heresy. On Friday the thirteenth, in October 1307, the king arrested five thousand of the knights who were too old to fight. He ordered them to be tortured to force confessions. The king eventually convinced Pope Clement V of their guilt, and the Knights Templar were abolished in 1312. Members who were not condemned were allowed to enter a similar group called the Order of Hospitallers.

The Papacy in Avignon

Ten years earlier, in 1302, Pope Boniface VIII had issued a papal bull, or edict. It stated that the pope held supreme power and stressed the obligation of all kingdoms to submit to him. But King Philip IV was not pleased with the stance the pope had taken. He burned the pope's document publicly in Paris. Philip also arranged to have the pope held captive, beaten, and nearly killed. Pope Boniface was rescued, but he died soon after. Then his successor, Pope Benedict XI, died after only eight months in office.

A conclave was held to elect a new pope. In the shadow of such terrible conflict, the political leaders of Europe tried to influence the bishops in their choice of a new head of the Church. The election was deadlocked. Pope Clement V, from France, was finally elected. But he refused to move to Rome. Instead, he moved the papacy to the city of Avignon in southern France. The pope and his officials felt safe and comfortable in Avignon. The papacy remained in Avignon for more than seventy years. While there, it was under the influence of the French monarchy. This was not good for the universal Church, which has its true center in Rome.

LATEST & GREATEST

The first alarm clocks were invented by intelligent ancient people, such as the Greek philosopher Plato (428–348 BC). He used a water drip/evaporation system to wake students for his early morning lectures. It wasn't until the latter part of the fourteenth century that a more practical and more accurate mechanical alarm clock was invented. The hands of this clock went around until they reached the desired hour. Then one hand hit a bar that rang a bell.

Mystery of History

What happened to the Anasazi? They were a Native American tribe that built the Palace of Mesa Verde in a cliff in Colorado. The whole society disappeared early in the fourteenth century. Find out more about these fascinating people and some of the reasons offered for their disappearance.

Saint Catherine of Siena and the Pope's Return to Rome

In 1376, Catherine of Siena (1347–1380) traveled to Avignon with a group of companions. She was intent on convincing Pope Gregory XI to return to the pope's rightful place in Rome. Although hesitant, Pope Gregory did agree. He made a triumphant entry into Rome in 1377. Saint Catherine, worn out by her prayers, fasting, and travels, died in 1380. It is thought that she died of a broken heart. This is because in the three short years that the papacy was back in Rome, a group of cardinals elected a second "pope" in Avignon. Others, in an attempt to correct this situation, elected a third "pope" in Pisa.

This was a period of great suffering for the Church. It is called the Great Western Schism, or Papal Schism, because of the terrible divisions it caused between believers. People were not sure which of the three men was the real pope. This problem would not be resolved until the fifteenth century. In the meantime, people no longer looked to the pope as the highest Christian authority. At this time in history, the emperor appeared more powerful than the pope.

On the Record

Saint Catherine of Siena (1347–1380) was a third order Dominican and mystic. She shouldered the responsibility of bringing the papacy from Avignon, France, back to Rome. Catherine wrote many letters encouraging the pope to return. Here is an excerpt from one to Pope Gregory XI:

"Come and do not resist God's will which calls you. The flock is starving and awaits your return to the place of your predecessor, Saint Peter. You are the Vicar of Christ and you must take up again your proper place. Come bravely, for God will be with you. Be comforted and fear nothing. I humbly ask your blessing … and beg pardon for my boldness."

John Wycliffe and John Hus

Two highly educated men latched onto the scandals and failings of Church leaders to call for reform. These men were John Wycliffe of England (1330–1384) and John Hus of Prague (1369–1415). Unfortunately, the good intentions that may have prompted them did not prevent them from taking their demands too far. Both men fell into heresy. Wycliffe denounced both clergy and sacraments; he began to teach that salvation was found only in Sacred Scripture. Hus held similar beliefs. He traveled to the Council of Constance to seek approval, but was arrested by the emperor and put to death.

ONCE UPON A WORD

Schism (SKIZ-uhm) is the sin of deliberately breaking away from the Church. This term comes from a Greek word meaning "split." The unity of believers is important. Because of this, any divisions in the Church are both serious and sad.

SNAPSHOT

Geoffrey Chaucer

Geoffrey (pronounced *Jeffrey*) Chaucer (around 1343–1400) is one of the most celebrated English poets of all time. He was the son of a wine merchant, but little else is known of his youth. As an adult he fought in the Hundred Years' War with France and had to be ransomed after being taken prisoner. Chaucer became a servant of the king and often went on diplomatic missions to France and Italy. In 1366 he married Philippa Roet, one of the queen's ladies-in-waiting. Together they had several children. To support his family, Chaucer had to work as a building project manager and as the royal forester. He was also a member of parliament. During these assignments Chaucer wrote his many poems. His best known work is *Canterbury Tales*, which he began in 1387. Written in the Middle English of his day, they are tales told by and about a group of thirty pilgrims traveling to the shrine of Saint Thomas à Becket in Canterbury. Although the charming and clever *Canterbury Tales* were never finished, they remain among the most important and beloved works of English literature. Geoffrey Chaucer, a devoted Catholic, died in 1400. He was the first poet to be buried in London's Westminster Abbey.

ACTIVITY

Chaucer's *Canterbury Tales* is a collection of stories told as a group of pilgrims walks together. Write or tell a poem or story about a trip you have taken or a journey you have made. Will your story be serious or funny? Will it be true, partly true, or completely fictional?

Prayer

God, our Father, please keep all of us faithful to the Church of your Son Jesus. Help us imitate the saints like Saint Catherine of Siena, who gave her whole life to God for the good of the Church. Inspire me to pray for the pope so that he may lead us to you. Remind me, too, to pray for unity within the Church. Amen.

The Bigger Picture

So many changes occurred in the fourteenth century that it is difficult to imagine what it was like to be alive at that time. There were numerous conflicting opinions about the roles of those in leadership—the popes and kings—and many new ideas about the place of ordinary people. For most, the questions of the day were difficult to answer. Should Christians follow those who taught that the pope had too much authority? Should they speak out about things that seemed wrong or false, like the accusations against the Knights Templar? Should they support Saint Catherine in bringing the pope back to Rome? Perhaps we would have been just as confused about what was right or wrong. One thing we can learn from back then, however, is the importance of taking advantage of the ways we have to be educated and informed.

In the fifteenth century we will be introduced to a very important invention for the sharing of information. That invention was the printing press, which allowed the publication of news to happen on a more regular schedule. This will not be the only "new" thing to happen, however. Culture, exploration, and invention will make great strides in the next hundred years as well.

Chapter 15

1403—The Chinese encyclopedia *Yung-lo Ta-tien* is begun. It comprised 22,937 manuscript rolls. Only three copies were produced.

AD 1412

AD 1424

AD 1436

1438—Incas rule Peru.

AD 1448

1450—The Vatican Library is founded.

1453—The Hundred Years' War between France and England ends.

1455—The Wars of the Roses take place in England (between the houses of York and Lancaster). They end in 1485 with the coronation of Henry VII, the first Tudor king.

AD 1460

1462—Ivan the Great becomes Grand Prince of Moscow.

AD 1472

AD 1484

1488—The Portuguese Bartolomeu Dias successfully sails around the Cape of Good Hope, the southern tip of Africa. About a decade later, Vasco da Gama rounds the cape and makes it all the way to India.

AD 1496

1493—Lands discovered in the New World are divided between Spain and Portugal by Pope Alexander VI.

A New World

In the last century we saw how the Church continued to struggle with heresy and division. Now we will see the Church try to rid herself of heresy once and for all. Leaders will work to reform how the Church governed itself. They will also seek to repair the Great Western Schism.

15th century

crowning of
Pope Martin V
in Constance on
November 11, 1417

The Council of Constance

Cardinals met in the German city of Constance for an ecumenical council from November 1414 to April 1418. Why was it held in Germany and not in Rome, or even in France, where the last few popes had lived? The reason might have had something to do with Emperor Sigismund. He had called for the council and was himself from Germany. The cardinals may have thought that Germany would prove to be a neutral place. Neither the French nor the Italian cardinals would have home-field advantage there.

Martin V

Too Many Popes

At the time the council was held, three different men were claiming to be pope. Only one had been rightfully elected. The other two are considered antipopes. The Council of Constance was able to end the schism by removing the two antipopes from office and accepting the true pope's resignation. Then the cardinals elected a new Holy Father, Pope Martin V.

Conciliarism

Because of the success the Council of Constance had in resolving the Great Schism, some cardinals began to think the Church should be led by councils rather than the pope. They proposed that the pope's title as head of the church be an honorary one. This idea, known as Conciliarism, was popular for a short time.

LATEST & GREATEST

Johannes Gutenberg (1398–1468) is credited with developing the printing press. That is because he was the first to perfect movable type. Movable type involved durable metal letters that could be arranged into words. Gutenberg filled trays with type on a wooden frame in the form of a page. Sheets of paper or vellum (calfskin parchment) were pressed against the pages. Once texts were printed, learning could be standardized. This, in turn, enabled more people to learn how to read. In 1452 Gutenberg printed fewer than 200 copies of a two-volume Latin Bible. His Bible was sold at the first international book fair in Frankfurt, Germany. It cost what a clerk would have been paid for three years of work. The Frankfurt book fair is still held every October!

A Brief Agreement

The Council of Florence (1438–1445) was also held during this fruitful time. There, bishops from the East and the West met to try to end the Eastern Schism. The Byzantine emperor and the patriarch of Constantinople even participated. Several agreements were reached. Rome would allow the Greek Church to keep its way of celebrating the liturgy. Representatives of the Greek Church agreed to a few compromises about the power of the pope, the teaching about purgatory, and the change that the Latin Church had made to the Creed (see page 100). Eventually, other Eastern Orthodox Churches joined the council as well. The reunification of the Church looked promising.

Unfortunately, the agreements never took effect. The proposed compromises were not welcomed by Orthodox clergy or laity back in Constantinople. After this disappointment, future popes decided to assume control over the councils. To show that the pope possessed this authority as Vicar of Christ and Successor of Saint Peter, only a handful of councils were called in the next 500 years.

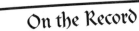

On the Record

Christopher Columbus made several voyages to the Americas. In this letter, he warmly describes the indigenous people he met:

"The inhabitants . . . are all, as I said before, unprovided with any sort of iron. They are destitute of arms, which are entirely unknown to them, and for which they are not adapted; not on account of any bodily deformity, for they are well made, but because they are timid and full of terror. [. . .] But when they see that they are safe, and all fear is banished, they are very guileless and honest, and very liberal of all they have. No one refuses the asker anything that he possesses; on the contrary, they themselves invite us to ask for it. They manifest the greatest affection toward all of us, exchanging valuable things for trifles, content with the very least thing or nothing at all. [. . .] I gave them many beautiful and pleasing things, which I had brought with me, for no return whatever, in order to win their affection, and that they might become Christians and inclined to love our King and Queen and Princes and all the people of Spain . . . ."

—from a letter to King Ferdinand and Queen Isabella of Spain, March 15, 1493

The Ottoman Empire

Any remaining hopes to reunify the Church were dashed in 1453; Constantinople was sacked by the Turks. Hagia Sophia (Holy Wisdom) Basilica, the mother church of Orthodox Christians, was taken over and turned into a mosque. This marked the fall of the Byzantine Empire and the rise of the Ottoman Empire. Muslims were now permanently in control.

The Renaissance

The popes were once again reigning from the holy city of Rome. They now turned their attention to art and culture. Beginning with Pope Nicholas V, who reigned from 1447 to 1455, a new age began for the Church. It is known as the *Renaissance* (REN-uh-sahns) or "rebirth." During the next hundred years, the creative expression of "beauty" was all the rage. The popes and many rich patrons—such as the Medici family of Florence, Italy—commissioned some of the best known and loved works of art, literature, architecture, and music ever created.

Nicolaus Copernicus

Nicolaus Copernicus (1473–1543) was an astronomer and mathematician. Born in the Polish town of Torún, he was also a Catholic priest. In his day people believed that the earth was the center of the universe. This had been the theory of the Egyptian astronomer, Ptolemy. Copernicus, however, believed that the sun was the center. According to him, the earth and the other planets revolved around the sun in a series of orbits. Copernicus laid out his theory in *Concerning the Revolutions of the Celestial Spheres* (1543). The scholarly world, as well as Church authorities, condemned his work as foolishness. To propose a heliocentric, or sun-centered, theory was contrary to common sense (what could be observed) and to the Bible (which speaks of the sun moving around the earth in Joshua 10:12–13). The year before his book was published, Copernicus fell ill and became paralyzed. It is said that the first printed pages of his book were presented to him just before he died.

Fra Angelico

da Vinci

Michelangelo

EWALD HANSER.

Art in the Church

Florence was the capital of the artistic renaissance. One of its most notable artists was Fra Angelico (1395–1455). He was known particularly for his frescos (wall paintings) of the life of Christ. Another prominent artist was Leonardo da Vinci (1452–1519). He was not only one of the best painters of history but also an inventor, an architect, and a mathematician. Da Vinci's best-known paintings are the *Mona Lisa* and *The Last Supper*. He also left notebooks of invaluable sketches, including his plan for a flying machine. His only equal was Michelangelo Buonarroti (1475–1564). Michelangelo was a sculptor, a painter, an engineer, and an architect. As a young man he had already created two of his best-known sculptures: the *Pietà* and *David*. Pope Julius II hired Michelangelo to paint biblical scenes on the ceiling of the Sistine Chapel at the Vatican. It took him four years. Michelangelo was also one of the architects responsible for finishing the largest church in the world—St. Peter's Basilica in Rome, with its famous dome.

Mystery of History

What is the Voynich Manuscript? The only thing really known about it is how old it is. The parchment it was written on has been carbon-dated to between 1400 and 1450. This means that the parchment has existed since that time. The manuscript has 116 leaves, or pages, covered with colored illustrations and charts. It was written in a totally unknown script, or language. For centuries experts have tried to decipher the mysterious alphabet; some believe is a code of some sort. Because of the illustrations, the book is thought to cover topics such as alchemy, botany, biology, astronomy, herbology, and cosmology. It is kept in the Beinecke Rare Book & Manuscript Library at Yale University.

Music in the Church

Two of the principal musicians of the fifteenth century were Johannes Ockeghem and Josquin des Prez. Ockeghem (around 1410–1497) was a Belgian composer, choirmaster, and singer. Des Prez (around 1450–1521) was also a composer from Belgium. Both were credited with writing music for Masses, beautifully harmonized religious pieces for choruses (motets), and songs. During the Renaissance a number of instruments familiar to us were developed. These include the guitar, the violin, the lute, and various keyboard instruments. And, thanks to Johannes Gutenberg's invention of the printing press, musicians were able to distribute copies of their compositions more widely.

des Prez

Ockeghem

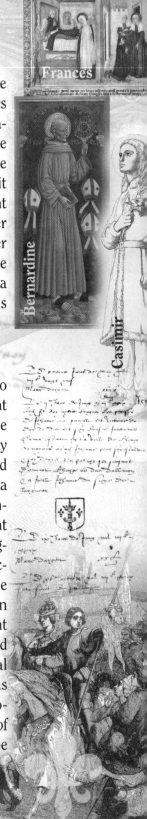

Some Saints of the 15th Century

As beautiful as art is, the most beautiful thing in the world created by God is the human spirit. This beauty shows itself in so many ways. Sometimes it is reflected in a charitable concern for those in need, as with Saint Frances of Rome (1384–1440). She formed a group of companions to serve the poor and sick of her city. Other times this beautiful spirit shines through examples of priestly service, as with Saint Bernardine of Siena (1380–1444). He was a great preacher who reformed the Franciscans and increased their number tenfold. Leaders of nations can also display the best of the human spirit, as did Saint Casimir (1458–1484). He was a Polish prince who refused to go to war out of respect for his enemies.

Saint Joan of Arc

But the Lord can also call someone to lead an army into war, as he did with Saint Joan of Arc (1412–1431). Joan was a simple peasant girl from northeast France. One day God sent Saint Michael the Archangel and Saint Catherine of Alexandria to give her a special mission. Joan was to personally convince the French prince to fight for his right to be king. Although she was just a teenager with no military training, Joan was successful in her military campaigns. After the prince was crowned King Charles VII, Joan was captured by her enemies. She underwent a long trial and was executed as a witch and a heretic. Twenty-one years later a new trial was held. The trial that condemned Joan was proclaimed a fraud. She was declared innocent and named a martyr in 1456. Joan of Arc was canonized on May 16, 1920, by Pope Benedict XV.

Ferdinand & Isabella

A United Spain

In Spain, lands that had been lost to the Muslims in previous centuries were being reconquered. For the first time, Spain was united as one Christian kingdom by the royal marriage of Ferdinand of Aragon and Isabella of Castille. The king and queen decided that in order to complete the reconquest of Spain, they needed to weed out traitors and heretics. In 1478, they began the Spanish Inquisition to do that.

The Spanish Inquisition

Unlike the inquisition of the twelfth century, the inquisition in Spain was controlled by the government, not the Church. The inquisitors were members of the clergy. They investigated the accusations of heresy, deciding whether or not someone was guilty. Punishment, however, was completely left up to state authorities.

In the fifteenth century, the use of torture was common throughout Europe. People accused of crimes had practically no rights. By the standards of the time, Spanish Inquisition trials were more fair and punishments less extreme than trials in the regular courts. Of the 40,000 people tried as heretics by the Spanish Inquisition, 40 were put to death.

There was corruption, however, and abuses did occur. For example, some Spaniards were jealous of the prosperity of the Jewish families who had converted to Christianity under pressure. These *conversos* were accused of only pretending to be Christian. Many were arrested and tried. Those who were "proven" to be false Christians forfeited their property and were forced to leave the kingdom. All Jews (about 200,000 people) were ultimately expelled from Spain in 1492.

Castle of Saint George: inquisitorial jail in Seville

Global Exploration

In the final decade of this century a great surge of exploration took place. Many brave men sailed from their homes in search of new lands and fortunes. We may be most familiar with the 1492 voyage of Christopher Columbus (1450–1506). Columbus sailed west from Spain in search of a new route to India. What he found instead were Caribbean islands just off the coast of a whole new world. (That's why we call them the *West Indies*!) In 1497 the Portuguese explorer Vasco da Gama (1460–1524) did find the way to India, by sailing around the southern tip of Africa.

That same year John Cabot (1450–1499), born in Italy as Giovanni Caboto, sailed across the Atlantic for King Henry VII of England. He came upon Canada and called it, appropriately, "Newfoundland." Cabot claimed all of North America for the English. Two years later, the Italian Amerigo Vespucci (1454–1512), financed by Spain, arrived in South America and discovered the great Amazon River. Pedro Cabral (1467–1520) made a similar trip in 1500; he claimed what is now Brazil for the Portuguese.

The world was expanding with all these discoveries. New lands called to the Church as Jesus did to his disciples: "Go out to the whole world and make disciples of all nations!" Almost all of the great explorers took missionary priests with them. Franciscan priest Juan Perez accompanied Christopher Columbus on his second voyage in 1493. The priest celebrated the first Mass in the Americas on December 8, the Feast of the Immaculate Conception, in what is now Haiti.

"My name is João and I serve the Portuguese prince, Henry I. Here in court the other boys and I hear about some of the most fantastic voyages men can make. His Majesty himself has sailed ships into the mysterious 'Dark Sea' of western Africa. He is the leader, or grand master, of the Military Order of Christ. People call him Henry the Navigator. When I am a man, I will also become an explorer for Portugal. I wonder what I will discover?"

ACTIVITY

Think of something that could be discovered or needs to be invented today, such as energy resources on other planets or a flying car. What is your idea? Do you know what it might take to actually create your invention or make your discovery? What questions would need to be answered?

Prayer

Dear Lord, I pray for artists, inventors, and discoverers of today. Help them pursue their ideas with enthusiasm and wisdom. May they receive the assistance they need from others to complete their work. May their goals be right and for the good of the human family. May they realize that their talents and abilities are gifts from you. And help me, too, to discover the gifts you have given me.
Amen.

The Bigger Picture

This chapter of history ends on a hopeful note. Many works of beauty have been created by the genius of artists and musicians. New lands are opening up for exploration and perhaps for colonization. These achievements make us appreciate the marvels of the human spirit.

In the next chapter we are going to see how important it is for us to be people of prayer. Then we will be open to God's Holy Spirit of wisdom, knowledge, and humility. We will also witness the importance of understanding and valuing what the Church teaches us. In the sixteenth century, some sincere people will try to reform the Church but will end up dividing it further. We know this next century as the time of the Protestant Reformation.

Chapter 16

1507—Martin Waldseemüller creates a world map using the name "America," in honor of Amerigo Vespucci, for the first time.

AD 1510

1513—Vasco Núñez de Balboa discovers the Pacific Ocean.
1517—Coffee is first brought to Europe.
1519—Hernán Cortés brings chocolate to Spain.

AD 1520

AD 1530

AD 1540

AD 1550

AD 1560

1564—The Russian reign of terror begins under Czar Ivan the Terrible.

AD 1570

AD 1580

1582—The Gregorian calendar (named for Pope Gregory XIII) is first adopted by Italy, Spain, and Portugal. In this year, October 4 is followed by October 15; ten days are removed.

1588—England's navy defeats the Spanish Armada.

AD 1590

1600—Shakespeare writes *Hamlet*.

164

Brothers Separate

Jesus founded one, and only one, Church. That is why divisions within the Church are so sad. What caused the breakup of the Christian Church in the sixteenth century? It wasn't disappointment with the teachings of Jesus. Divisions began with the misinterpretation of Church teachings by some individuals and errors in judgment by others. Because of the printing press, wrong ideas spread quickly throughout Europe and gained popular support.

These events, coupled with the political ambition of kings, caused a great storm within the Church. Those who protested against the Catholic Church saw this century as a chance to reform and purify certain religious practices. Those who remained loyal Catholics saw these efforts as a revolt against their faith—one that damaged the unity Jesus intended for the Church.

16th century

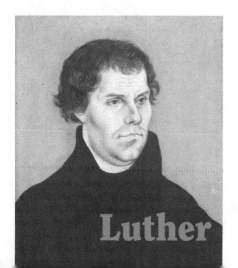

Luther

Martin Luther

The best known of the "reformers" was a German Augustinian monk named Martin Luther (1483–1546). Luther was ordained a priest in 1507. He was a biblical scholar at the University of Wittenberg in Germany. Somewhere along the way, Luther began

to question the leadership structure of the Church and what she taught about the sacraments. He was also disturbed by a practice he considered corrupt: indulgences. (An indulgence is the complete or partial cancellation of the punishment due for sin. The Church grants indulgences for specific good actions or prayers. An indulgence may be gained for oneself or for someone who has died.) At this time in history, abuses were creeping in. Indulgences were being promoted and promised in exchange for donations toward the building fund for the new St. Peter's Basilica in Rome.

In 1517 Luther wrote his protest, *Ninety-five Theses*, and nailed it to the door of the Castle Church. The theses were a list of points meant to challenge the Church to reform. Unfortunately, Luther's *Ninety-five Theses* also departed from the truths of the Catholic faith. He wrote that the Bible was the *only* word of God and that *only* Sacred Scripture—and not Sacred Tradition—had authority. Luther also taught that people were saved by faith *alone*; good works had no value when it came to salvation.

These views were condemned by Church leaders as heresies. They questioned Luther about his teachings and tried to bring him back into union with the faith of the Church. Their efforts ultimately failed. Luther left the priesthood and the Augustinians and married. Along with his followers, he left the Roman Catholic Church and formed his own church. Later, it came to be known as the Lutheran Church.

Erasmus

Zwingli

Calvin

Knox

Reformers Inside and Out

Desiderius Erasmus (1467–1536) was a Dutch philosopher. His writings were highly critical of some Church practices at the time. They set the stage for the Reformation. Erasmus sincerely longed for true reform, but *within* the Church. He was disappointed by the outcome of the Protestant Reformation.

Other reformers were at work throughout Europe at the time. Today we recognize names like Huldrych Zwingli (1484–1531) and John Calvin (1509–1564) in Switzerland, and John Knox (1514–1572) in England and Scotland. These men took advantage of the dissatisfaction stirred up by Martin Luther. They put forth their own ideas and demands for change. All of them separated from the Roman Catholic Church. They were called Protestants because they held beliefs that protested official Church teachings.

It is true that the sixteenth-century Church needed a better understanding of its teachings and practices. These reforms, however, could have been accomplished *within* the Church. Reformers could have followed the examples of saints such as Pope Gregory the Great, Saint Francis of Assisi, and Saint Catherine of Siena. It is a tragedy that the men who might have inspired new holiness and goodness inside the Church chose to turn away from her instead.

Politics and the Reformation

The idea of reforming the Church also fed a growing political discontent in much of Europe. Those who sought reform could have worked for change by submitting their ideas to a council or directly to the pope. Instead, they were often used by local princes and others to gain power and further their own political purposes.

Many nobles saw the Reformation as an opportunity to free themselves from the Church's influence. Protestant princes were no longer under the authority of the bishop or pope. They simply stopped listening to any guidance the Church gave them. Even worse, subjects were expected to belong to the same church their ruler did. Ordinary people were pressured to choose between their Catholic faith and remaining in the lands their families had lived in for generations.

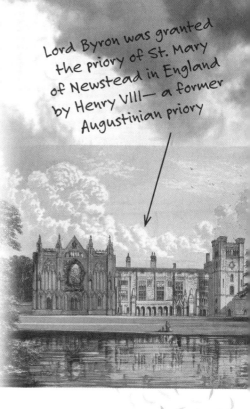

Lord Byron was granted the priory of St. Mary of Newstead in England by Henry VIII— a former Augustinian priory

LATEST & GREATEST

Pencils are well known to students, especially the common yellow #2 pencils used for doing math problems and taking standardized tests. Ancient Romans used a disk of lead to draw with, and a rod of lead, called a stylus, to write with. They might also use a thin brush called a *penicillum*.

In a storm in 1564 a large tree blew over in the English town of Borrowdale. People noticed a very hard, dark substance in the ground. They assumed it was lead, but it was found to be pure black carbon. It could be cut in strips and wrapped in string, wood, or skins, then used for marking things. The people of Borrowdale used it to put identifying marks on their sheep. In time, someone decided to call the carbon "graphite," based on the Greek word for writing, because it made writing easy. And so was born the writing instrument known as the graphite pencil.

Henry VIII and Saint Thomas More

The year 1521 was an important one for young King Henry VIII (1491–1547) of England. Henry opposed Luther's rebellion against the Church. In fact, he wrote a book on the importance and power of the sacraments as a way to counter Protestant teaching. In gratitude the Vatican gave Henry the title Defender of the Faith.

But by 1529 the king was desperate for a son and heir. He was also unfaithful to his wife, Catherine of Aragon. Henry wanted to annul his marriage to the queen and marry a younger woman, Anne Boleyn, instead. But his chancellor, Cardinal Wolsey (1475–1530), failed to get Pope Clement VII's permission for the divorce. So Henry replaced him with a well-respected lawyer, Sir Thomas More (1478–1535).

More, however, was a faithful Catholic. In 1532, he decided to resign his position as Lord Chancellor rather than agree to the king's divorce. In 1533, King Henry cut England off from the authority of Rome. He obtained a decree from Archbishop Thomas Cranmer of Canterbury nullifying his marriage to Queen Catherine. Henry then married Anne Boleyn. The king was excommunicated by Pope Paul III in 1538.

With the help of his new chancellor, Sir Thomas Audley, an Act of Supremacy was drafted. It declared that King Henry was head of the Church in England. Everyone was expected to accept this outrageous claim to power. Thomas More's good conscience would not allow him to sign this act. Because

Henry VIII

Catherine

Anne

Wolsey

Thomas More

On the Record

Sir Thomas More was faithful to the Catholic faith. He refused to sign the Act of Supremacy declaring King Henry VIII head of the Church in England. After he was condemned to death he spoke these words to his judges:

"... I verily trust ... that we may hereafter meet joyfully together in Heaven to our everlasting Salvation: and God preserve you, especially my sovereign lord the King, and grant him faithful counselors."

Sir Thomas More was beheaded on July 6, 1535. Right before he died he declared for all to hear: "I am the king's good servant, but God's first."

of this, he was imprisoned in the Tower of London and put to death in 1535.

Henry VIII went from bad to worse. He stole all the monasteries and other Church properties, imprisoned priests, and married and divorced several more wives. He even executed two of them. Strangely, with all the destruction Henry VIII did to the Catholic Church in England, he did not alter the teachings or practice of the faith. His motivation was personal power, not reformation.

Henry died in 1547. His only son, Edward VI, died at age 15. Henry's oldest daughter, Mary, became queen in 1553 and restored England to union with Rome. Five years later, Henry's second daughter became queen. She reigned as Elizabeth I for almost fifty years, from 1558 to 1603. Elizabeth was the daughter of Anne Boleyn. It was not surprising that she declared herself head of the Church of England and returned the country to Protestantism.

The Council of Trent

Pope Paul III called for an Ecumenical Council in 1537. Political squabbles, however, kept it from occurring until 1545. At the Council of Trent, the pope wanted to find ways to respond to the Protestant Reformation. How should the Church address the concerns reformers had raised? How could Church teaching be made clearer? And how could these new divisions be reconciled?

The council was held in several sessions from 1545 to 1563. Protestant leaders were invited to attend but refused to come. It was too late to heal the divisions that had already existed for forty years. Trent was really a council of clarification. Its rulings set the tone of Catholic life for the next three hundred years. The council stressed a number of teachings: that salvation depends on faith *and* good works; that our faith is based on the Bible *and* tradition; that the interpretation of the Bible belongs to the Church; that there are seven sacraments; that the Mass is a sacrifice *and* a meal; and that Jesus Christ is truly present in the Eucharist. The council fathers decided to require each diocese to have a seminary to train its priests; to regulate the use of indulgences; to prepare a new catechism; and to publish new liturgical books, including the Missal and the Breviary.

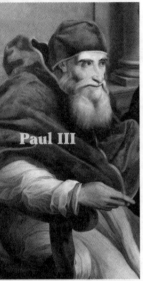

Paul III

Saint Ignatius of Loyola

These were years of many saints. Some were martyrs, others were reformers in their own right. We could talk about any one of these saints: Charles Borromeo, Robert Bellarmine, John of the Cross, Francis Xavier, Margaret Clitherow, Teresa of Avila, or Philip Neri. Each was important in the history of the Catholic Church. But we will focus on someone who was a soldier-saint: Ignatius of Loyola (1491–1556).

Iñigo Lopez de Loyola was born in Spain in 1491. As a child, Iñigo dreamed of becoming a great knight. He joined the army while still a young man. After suffering a leg wound

Teresa of Avila

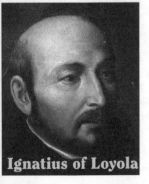

Ignatius of Loyola

while fighting a battle in 1521, Iñigo went home to recover. To while away the time he read the only books he could find: the Bible and the lives of the saints. The stories touched his knight's heart; he realized that heroism could be found in following Christ.

Iñigo completed his studies and asked to be ordained. He spent time reflecting on God's call. Soon he gathered friends together and formed the Company of Jesus, known to us as the Society of Jesus (Jesuits). For his new calling Iñigo chose a new name for himself: Ignatius. His religious family put itself completely at the service of the pope. The Holy Father would send them all over the world: to South America, Canada, Ethiopia, India, China, Congo, and throughout Europe. The Jesuits were missionaries and extraordinary educators. By the time Saint Ignatius died, there were nearly 1,000 Jesuits serving as soldiers of Christ.

ONCE UPON A WORD

A *mercenary* is someone who hires himself out, particularly as a soldier. Mercenaries are also called soldiers of fortune. They fight for pay or some other advantage, rather than out of loyalty or for a country or cause they believe in.

SNAPSHOT

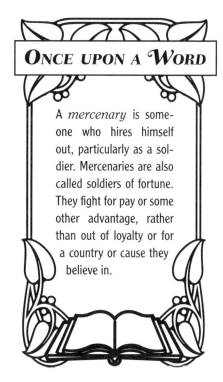

Matteo Ricci

Christian missionaries to China had found little success among the people there. In 1582, the Jesuits decided to try a new approach. They sent Father Matteo Ricci (1552–1610) and another priest to Macao to study Chinese language and customs. The two men brought many Western curiosities with them, including clocks, sundials, and maps of the world. These things drew other intellectuals to their home for discussions. Encouraged by the friendships they formed, the two priests translated a catechism into Chinese. It took the form of a conversation between a Chinese man and a European priest. It was well received.

By 1588 Father Ricci was on his own. The second priest had returned to Italy to gain support for the new mission, but he had died there. Building on their successes, Ricci began dressing like a Chinese scholar. Soon he was invited to move to the capital city of Beijing. There he enjoyed great prestige and gained respect for the "Western God" he served.

Matteo Ricci is unique among European Christian missionaries. He adopted the culture of the people he was trying to reach. Father Ricci showed how faith in Christ is truly universal.

The Swiss Guard

The world's smallest army was formed in 1506. A corps of Swiss mercenaries, or soldiers for hire, was installed in Rome to protect the pope. Swiss soldiers had been renowned throughout Europe for several centuries. They were considered the bravest and best-trained soldiers in the world. The original group of 150 Swiss Guards met their first big test when the Holy Roman Emperor Charles V attacked Rome in 1527. In a desperate attempt to hold off the imperial troops, more than one hundred Swiss Guards were killed. Only the survivors who had been escorting Pope Clement VII to safety were spared.

Along with the lives of the brave guards who died, Rome lost many treasures of art and an enormous amount of gold. Unfortunately, the pope had angered both the emperor and the French king, Francis I. Now he was forced to surrender to the emperor and spend some months as a prisoner. In the end, Pope Clement had to give up several of the cities of the Papal States in order to gain some degree of freedom.

The Swiss Guard still serve at the Vatican today. Known for their colorful uniforms, their job is to protect the pope and the Church. Not just anyone can be a member of the guard. Applicants must be unmarried Swiss citizens and Roman Catholics with good morals. They must be at least 5-foot-8 ½-inches tall, between 19 and 30 years of age, and have a professional or high school diploma. Members of the Swiss Guard attend military school in Switzerland.

Charles V

Clement VII

Swiss Guard now & then

John of Austria

The Battle of Lepanto

Divisions caused by the Protestant Reformation didn't make it any easier to deal with the Muslim advance against Europe. Muslims armies and navies had set their sights on Venice and eventually Rome. To gain such a prize, however, they needed to control the Mediterranean Sea.

Pope Saint Pius V (1566–1572) realized that a very large navy was needed. He approached friends and foes alike and convinced them of the urgency of joining forces. The Holy League was formed. It was made up of battleships from Spain, Malta, Tuscany, Savoy, Venice, and the papal fleet. A young but experienced man named John of Austria was appointed to lead the league fleet.

One of the most spectacular naval victories in history happened on October 7, 1571. This was when a Christian fleet of 200 ships defeated the larger Ottoman Turk fleet of 300 ships in the Battle of Lepanto. The two navies faced each other off the coast of Greece. The Christian sailors were encouraged to pray the Rosary in preparation for battle. For a time, it seemed that the Muslim fleet would be victorious.

Then the Spanish admiral went to pray before a miraculous image of Mary entrusted to his ship. It was a copy of Our Lady of Guadalupe. This was the image Mary had imprinted on the *tilma* of the Mexican peasant Juan Diego forty years earlier, in 1531. When the admiral finished praying, the winds turned in favor of the league vessels. They raced toward the Muslim fleet; in a few hours they managed to completely destroy it. The Muslim navy lost 30,000 men that day, while the league lost only 7,000. Nearly 10,000 Christian galley slaves were freed from enemy ships as well. This great victory was attributed to Mary's intercession.

At the very moment of victory, Pope Pius V sensed the outcome. He told his advisers that they needed to stop their meeting and give praise to God for Mary's great victory. In gratitude to Mary, Pope Pius established a feast in honor of Our Lady of Victory on October 7. The next pope, Gregory XIII, changed the name of the feast to Our Lady of the Rosary.

Mystery of History

The fate of English colonists at Roanoke Island, in North Carolina, has been a mystery since their disappearance in 1590. The colonists had made two previous landings at the site. Explorers arrived first in 1584. The next year soldiers came to stake their claim to land. The third group of 118 people arrived in 1587; it included families coming to settle. But when the next ship arrived in 1590, there was no sign of the colonists. The only clues left behind were the word "Croatoan," which someone had carved in a gatepost, and the letters "Cro" on a nearby tree.

Some fear that a disaster befell the colony, such as disease, drought, or even a hurricane. Others think that the community may have sought protection from attackers by fleeing to a friendly tribe of Native Americans called Croatons. What do you think? Do some research and see what you can discover to help solve this mystery.

"I am Pepe, a servant in the house of Bishop Zumárraga of Mexico City. On December 12, 1531, I saw Juan Diego coming to see His Excellency. He had come twice before. I went right away to get him a cup of water. As I entered the room for visitors, I saw the bishop kneeling in front of Juan Diego! He looked so amazed. I moved around to see why and saw the beautiful image of Our Lady on Juan Diego's *tilma* (cloak). Roses lay all around on the floor. My heart was beating so fast when I noticed the Lady's face. Our Lady of Guadalupe is an Aztec like me. She is truly our mother and Mother of the Americas."

I Witness

Explorers, Soldiers, Missionaries

Countries were driven by the thirst for discovery. Their restlessness found an outlet in exciting journeys of exploration. Explorers, soldiers, and missionaries all set out. Among them was the Spanish explorer Juan Ponce de Leon, who sailed from Puerto Rico to Florida in 1513; Ferdinand Magellan, whose voyage circumnavigated the globe; Aleixo Garcia, who spent years traveling through present-day Brazil, Paraguay, and Bolivia; Francisco Pizarro, who explored Peru, Ecuador, and the Incan Empire; Jacques Cartier of France, who explored Canada by way of the St. Lawrence River; and the Dutchman Willem Barents, who explored the Northern waters until he died there after spending a winter with his ship frozen in the ice.

Explorers were often followed by military expeditions. Hernán Cortés (1485–1547) came to Mexico as a *conquistador*, a "conquerer," in 1519. His army defeated the Aztec ruler Montezuma. Cortés claimed the vast city of Tenochtitlán, today's Mexico City, for Spain. Like many soldiers who came to the Americas for the purpose of conquest, Cortés was a brutal foe. Native peoples were often treated with disrespect and even violence.

Francis Xavier

While explorers and soldiers traveled to foreign lands searching for wealth or power, the Church went in search of souls. Most explorers and armies brought along missionary priests. They took care of the spiritual needs of the Europeans they accompanied. They also worked to bring Christian faith to the peoples of the new world and the Far East. Some indigenous people were receptive to the Gospel message; others opposed it. Many missionary priests and brothers were persecuted or martyred. The risks, however, did not lessen their enthusiasm or dedication.

Spanish Franciscan and Dominican missionaries had great success with the native people of the Philippines. Schools, hospitals, vocational institutions, and even a university were founded by 1590. Perhaps one of the greatest missionaries of all times was the Jesuit, Saint Francis Xavier. He preached the Christian message to thousands. First he traveled to Goa, India; then to Malacca; and then to Japan. Francis Xavier died in 1552 on the island of Sancian (Shangchuan), while awaiting a ship to China.

More than the Facts

In almost every picture of St. Peter's Square in Vatican City we see a magnificent obelisk. Amazingly, this needle-shaped monument originated in ancient Egypt. It was transported to Rome by Emperor Caligula in 37 AD and placed at the Vatican Circus. The obelisk was likely one of the last things Saint Peter saw when he was crucified there. In 1586, Pope Sixtus V had the huge granite obelisk moved to its present location within the square in front of St. Peter's Basilica. This final move was directed by the Italian engineer Domenico Fontana. It is said that he employed up to 900 men and 150 horses, along with miles of rope, to move and lift the 330-ton monument into place. The obelisk stands eighty-three feet high from top to base. It has been positioned so as to act as a gigantic sun dial.

Prayer

Dear God, your Son taught us the importance of being one in mind and heart with you.
Jesus said: *Be one as the Father and I are
one.* Keep me from being divisive in any way.
Help me to be humble about the opinions I hold
and kind to those who disagree with me. Show
me how to be a child of unity and peace, always
faithful and proud of my Catholic faith.
Amen.

The Bigger Picture

The whole Western world was caught up in turmoil due to the Protestant Reformation. The sixteenth century was marked by events such as the Peasants' Revolt (1524–1525) in Germany and other popular uprisings. Many people sought to limit the secular control of the emperor and the religious power of the papacy. Nations were growing in a spirit of independence and gaining a national identity. They no longer saw themselves as part of a larger empire. And because of the Protestant Reformation, they were no longer able to see each other as members of the same Church.

Rulers sponsored expeditions to expand their influence and enrich themselves by conquest. Sadly, these goals were often pursued with cruelty and terrible injustice. Meanwhile, the Church set in motion a vast spiritual, educational, and cultural movement; it was known as the Counter-Reformation.

In the seventeenth century we will encounter significant historical changes. They will transform how people think about themselves as citizens of the vast global community of the Church.

Chapter 17

AD 1610 — 1609—The Dutch East India Company ships the first Chinese tea to Europe.

1611—The King James Bible is published in England during the reign of James I.

AD 1620

1626—The Dutch West India Company buys Manhattan Island from the Native Americans for $24 worth of merchandise.

AD 1630

1635—Latin Grammar School, the oldest high school in North America, is founded in Boston. Today it is known as Boston Latin School.

AD 1640

1642—The city of Montreal, Canada is founded as Ville Marie.

1644—The Ming Dynasty ends in China, replaced by the Qing—also known as Manchu—Dynasty.

1645—The Dalai Lama's residence is built in Lhasa, Tibet.

AD 1650

AD 1660

1661—French King Louis XIV, called "the sun king," assumes control of the government.

1666—Isaac Newton discovers the law of gravity.

1668—Rembrandt paints his "Return of the Prodigal Son."

AD 1670

AD 1680

1685—Johann Sebastian Bach, the great German composer, is born.

1689—Peter the Great becomes czar of Russia.

AD 1690

Game Changers

English Colonization of the Americas

Spanish Colonization of the Americas

Dutch and French Colonization of the Americas

Missionaries to the Americas

Saint Kateri Tekakwitha

Catholicism in the American Colonies

Catholicism in England

The Church in Japan

Queen Christina of Sweden

Saint Margaret Mary Alacoque

The Defeat of the Ottoman Empire

In this book we have seen much Christian history—sixteen centuries, to be exact—but are just coming to the beginnings of Church history in North America. Doesn't that seem amazing?

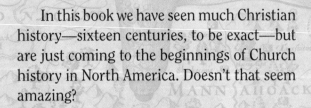

17th century

during her captivity by the English, Pocahantas converted to Christianity and took the name Rebecca

English Colonization of the Americas

English settlers came to Jamestown, Virginia in 1607. They had a few difficult years due to poor water supply, drought, and sickness. They also had a troubled relationship with the Powhatan Indians, in whose territory the English had settled. By the mid-1600s their fortunes had improved, however. Tobacco crops flourished, more settlers arrived, and a governor was installed. Sadly, the first African slaves arrived in 1619.

Another group of English investors followed the Jamestown settlement. They sent a ship that carried a group of religious people we know as the Pilgrims. The Pilgrims

On the Record

Mayflower Compact

"In ye name of God Amen· We whose names are vnderwriten, the loyall subjects of our dread soueraigne Lord King James by ye grace of God, of great Britaine, franc, & Ireland king, defender of ye faith, &c.

"Haueing vndertaken, for ye glorie of God, and aduancemente of ye christian faith and honour of our king & countrie, a voyage to plant ye first colonie in ye Northerne parts of Virginia· doe by these presents solemnly & mutualy in ye presence of God, and one of another, couenant, & combine our selues togeather into a ciuill body politick; for ye our better ordering, & preseruation & furtherance of ye ends aforesaid; and by vertue hearof, to enacte, constitute, and frame shuch just & equall lawes, ordinances, Acts, constitutions, & offices, from time to time, as shall be thought most meete & conuenient for ye generall good of ye colonie: vnto which we promise all due submission and obedience. In witnes wherof we haue herevnder subscribed our names at Cap Codd ye ·11· of Nouember, in ye year of ye raigne of our soueraigne Lord king James of England, france, & Ireland ye eighteenth and of Scotland ye fiftie fourth. Ano: Dom 1620"

were a small group of Protestants from the English Separatist Church. They had been persecuted by other Protestants, members of the Church of England. Their ship, the Mayflower, missed its original destination near New York's Hudson River. Instead it laid anchor in Plymouth Bay, near present-day Cape Cod, Massachusetts in 1620. Before disembarking, the pilgrims gave their colony a government by creating the Mayflower Compact. They struggled through the winter but survived with the assistance of the Wampanoag tribe. Over the next few decades the Pilgrims labored to maintain their independence. In 1691 they became part of the Massachusetts Bay Colony.

"Hello, my name is Jebediah. My great-grandparents came to New England on the Mayflower. Now the men in my family are whalers. The ships go out and hope to make a kill. Because whales are so enormous, they provide many things we need, especially oil for our lamps. I wonder if the ocean will run out of whales. I heard the elders say that the countries that supplied animals for Nero's games at the Coliseum killed many of them. I hope the ocean will never run out of whales."

I Witness

Spanish Colonization of the Americas

The English were not the first to colonize the New World. The Spanish had already founded successful settlements in present-day Haiti in 1493; in Santo Domingo in 1496; and in Venezuela in 1500. Activities in Mexico totally transformed the area. A series of Spanish settlements was established during the first decades of the sixteenth century. Over the next two centuries the Spanish continued their conquest and colonization in South and Central America.

Dutch and French Colonization of the Americas

In 1614 the Dutch settled in what are now parts of New York, New Jersey, Delaware, Connecticut, and Pennsylvania. French explorer Jacques Cartier planted a cross on the shores of the Gaspé Peninsula (now in eastern Quebec Province) in 1534. But other than a small number of fishermen, French colonies got off to a slow start.

In 1608, however, Samuel de Champlain successfully established a community in Quebec; three years later he did the same thing in Montreal. A profitable fur trade began to grow around these areas. These were repeated in places we know as Green Bay, Wisconsin in 1634 and Sault Ste. Marie, Ontario in 1668. A series of forts and trading posts appeared along the Mississippi and Saint Lawrence rivers.

ONCE UPON A WORD

Nepotism is the practice of showing favoritism to a relative when hiring or voting. *Simony* is the selling of holy things for profit.

Samuel de Champlain

SNAPSHOT

Marquette and Joliet

Father Jacques Marquette (1637–1675) was a French Jesuit priest who taught in the colleges of France until 1666. He then traveled to the New World as a missionary to the First Nations in and around Quebec. Father Marquette became fluent in the Huron language. He was later sent to a French settlement in the area of Michigan. From there he and Louis Joliet (1645–1700), a French-Canadian explorer, went with five companions on a canoe trip in search of the mouth of the Mississippi River. The French governor who sent them hoped it led to the Pacific Ocean. The group made their way to Green Bay, then the Fox River, then the Wisconsin River, and finally to the Mississippi. They came within a ten-day traveling distance to the Gulf of Mexico. The tribes they initially encountered on their trip were friendly. They were warned, however that if they continued they would find unfriendly tribes, as well as Spanish settlers. Rather than risk being captured by enemies of France, Marquette and Joliet decided to turn around. Joliet returned to Quebec, while Marquette set up a mission among the American Indians of Illinois who had been kind to the explorers.

Missionaries to the Americas

Sponsoring nations profited greatly from all the exploration and colonization. They gained new trade routes, gold and silver, lumber, prestige, and influence. Christian rulers too, both Catholic and Protestant, viewed the colonies as ways to spread Christian faith to the native peoples of the New World.

Eight Jesuit missionaries were among the most remarkable Catholic evangelizers of our continent. They worked among the Hurons in Ontario, Canada and upper New York State. These Jesuit priests, brothers, and lay volunteers were courageous and determined. They chose to remain in the New World despite the distrust of some of the Hurons and the hatred of the nearby Iroquois. In the middle of the century all of these missionaries met with martyrdom: Saint René Goupil in 1642; Saints Isaac Jogues and Jean de Lalande in 1646; Saint Antoine Daniel in 1648; and Saints Jean de Brébeuf, Noël Chabanel, Charles Garnier, and Gabriel Lalemant in 1649. These missionaries are known as the North American Martyrs or the Canadian Martyrs. As a result of the preaching and example of these martyrs, and the missionaries who followed them, many American First Nations embraced the faith.

Isaac Jogues

Jean de Brébeuf

Gabriel Lalemant

Kateri

Saint Kateri Tekakwitha

The most outstanding convert was Kateri Tekakwitha (1656–1680), the first North American saint. Kateri was the orphaned daughter of a Christian Algonquin mother and a Mohawk father from present upstate New York. When smallpox claimed her parents and brother, Kateri was taken in by an uncle's family. In 1666, their village was destroyed and they moved to the Mohawk village of Caughnawaga, where they lived for the next ten years. There Kateri met Jesuit missionaries, was instructed in the Catholic faith, and baptized. Her uncle's family disapproved and others could not understand why she embraced Christianity. They frequently bullied her and made life difficult for her, so Kateri fled to the Jesuit mission Kahnawake in Canada. Many other native people lived the Christian faith there. Kateri was now able to pray freely and spend her life in works of charity. In 1679 she received permission to make a vow of perpetual virginity. When she died, God seemed to give witness to her holy life by causing the scars of smallpox to disappear from her face. Many miracles have been attributed to her intercession. Kateri Tekakwitha was canonized in 2012.

LATEST & GREATEST

The calculator was invented in 1623 by German-born Wilhelm Schickard (1592–1635). He was an inventor, astronomer, mathematician, engraver, and mapmaker. Letters exist from Schickard to the astronomer Johannes Kepler (1571–1630), in which he explained his machine's usefulness in calculating astronomical tables. It was capable of adding and subtracting six-digit figures. In order to work multiplication and division, Schickard installed a device known as Napier's bones. This was invented by the Scotsman John Napier (1550–1617). The device included strips of bones that were engraved with series of numbers. Calculations were done as the individual bones moved in relation to one another.

Catholicism in the American Colonies

Catholics were not warmly welcomed in the early English-speaking American colonies. This intolerance was a consequence of the Protestant Reformation. From 1630 to 1632 George Calvert, Lord Baltimore, sought from King Charles I a charter for land. Calvert wanted to create the Catholic colony of Maryland. The charter passed five weeks after Calvert's death. His son, Cecilius, invited the first colonists. They included priests for the Catholics and ministers for the Protestants, who also came to settle there. In 1649, with the Act of Toleration, the colony in Maryland became the first whose governance was based on religious tolerance. However, things were not as easy as they seem. Throughout the century the colony faced attacks—both physical and legal—as the Virginia colony and English authorities tried to destroy this haven for Catholics in the New World.

George Calvert

Catholicism in England

In 1673 a law called the Test Act was in place in England. It kept Roman Catholics from holding any public offices in the country. Five years later, in 1678, a plan was made to end any tolerance of Catholics in the English court. King Charles II was not a Catholic but his queen was. So too were certain members of his court. Some Catholics tried to compromise. They looked for a way to promise their allegiance to the king without surrendering their loyalty to the Church. The Jesuit priests who were chaplains at court refused to make any compromise. They were accused of plotting to assassinate the king by Titus Oates, a renegade priest who was angry with the Church. This "Popish Plot" was seized upon by the enemies of the Church. They had the Jesuits and other priests arrested and either imprisoned or executed. Although this was a heavy blow to the Catholics in England, priests continued to arrive secretly by way of France to minister in the kingdom.

Charles II

CAROLUS STUART de II⁴
Koninck van
ENGELAND, SCOT...

King

D'Oates discovereth ŷ Plot
to ŷ King and Councell.

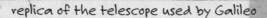

replica of the telescope used by Galileo

Mystery of History

Why is there so often conflict between the teachings of scientists and the beliefs of the Church?

One example dates from the seventeenth century. The Church opposed Galileo Galilei's theory that the earth revolves around the sun. This idea had first been shared by Copernicus. Galileo, an Italian physicist and astronomer, made many observations of the heavens through a telescope. Through his observations of the moon and tides, Galileo suggested that we live in a helio-centric universe (centered around the sun). Today we accept the centrality of the sun to our solar system; in the seventeenth century, however, science was still developing. It was just beginning to become a cultural force.

In Galileo's time the Bible was understood in a very literal way. Most edu-cated people believed, as we still do, that the Scriptures reveal God's truth. But they also assumed that the Bible was scientifically accurate. Because of this, even Pope Urban VIII, who had been a friend of Galileo, believed he was wrong and was concerned that his theories would lead people away from the truth. Galileo was put on trial in 1632. He was found guilty of false teaching and put under house arrest. Some people think Galileo's condemnation was more about politics than science. Galileo was a strong-willed man who often got into clashes with other scientists. Perhaps jealousy was the real reason for his punishment. Others believe that the Church was trying to stem the

influence of the powerful Medicis. This family had great wealth and power, and they backed Galileo's research.

Whatever the case, in the year 2000 Pope John Paul II issued a formal apology to Galileo on behalf of the Catholic Church.

The Church in Japan

Saint Francis Xavier had seen great promise for the Church in Japan when he arrived there in the sixteenth century. Even though local officials opposed the Church, many people had requested baptism. The number of Christians grew to 200,000 strong. Fortunately, Japanese Christians remained faithful when a series of religious persecutions began. Soon property was taken away, churches were destroyed, and missionaries were exiled. Still the Church continued to grow.

Just prior to the seventeenth century, however, an especially deadly persecution began. It was sparked by the discovery of weapons on a Spanish ship arriving from the Philippines. Panic seized Japanese authorities. Because Christianity had come from the West, Christians were suspected of being part of a Spanish plot to take over Japan. Many Christians were martyred; at times whole families died together. In Nagasaki, twenty-six missionaries and lay persons, including two children, were killed. The joy they expressed despite their suffering amazed even their executioners.

Persecutions steadily rose from 1614 on. It seemed Christianity had been wiped out. However, in 1854, when U.S. Commodore Matthew Perry made his way to Japan, he discovered Christians still practicing the faith in secret. Ten years later missionaries reported finding 20,000 Christians living their faith secretly on the island of Kyushu.

Christina of Sweden

Margaret Mary

Queen Christina of Sweden

Queen Christina of Sweden (1626–1689) was a well-educated woman, a patron of the arts, and a respected leader. She shocked the world in 1653 when she gave up her throne to embrace the Roman Catholic religion. Swedish law decreed that only a Lutheran could occupy the throne, so the queen designated a cousin as her successor and retired to Rome. Such a law may seem unusual to us today, but it illustrates how close Church and state were at that point in history.

Saint Margaret Mary Alacoque

We might wonder what Jesus thought during the years of wars and persecutions affecting his Church. In 1673, he offered an answer. Jesus began a series of appearances to a French sister of the Visitation of Holy Mary named Margaret Mary Alacoque (1647–1690). In these visits Jesus presented his Sacred Heart. He charged Sister Margaret Mary to make devotion to his heart known in the Church. Jesus wanted us to remember that he also lived a human life and that he understood our suffering. He asked us all to offer our sufferings as reparation for the sins that are committed. In this way, Jesus let us know that the sufferings of this life are joined with his sufferings and death on the cross. The Sacred Heart of Jesus shows us that human history has meaning and value.

John III Sobieski

Peter the Great

The Defeat of the Ottoman Empire

In 1683 the Ottoman Turks tried to besiege Vienna, Austria. Once they added this great city to their empire, they would march on Rome. The fortress in Vienna was massive, however, so the siege was taking longer than Sultan Mehmed IV had expected. Meanwhile, King John III Sobieski of Poland was advancing with an army of 60,000 troops from the Holy League. They surprised the Ottoman forces by attacking from a densely forested mountain. The victory for the Christian forces was complete and the Ottoman army was defeated. Although the sultan escaped, the threat to Europe ended. In 1696 the Russians stopped the further spread of Islam when Peter the Great defeated the Muslim forces in the Black Sea. This loss caused them to give up control of a large portion of Eastern Europe.

More than the Facts

The dodo (*Raphus cucullatus*) was a flightless bird related to the pigeon and the dove. Native to the island of Mauritius, it became extinct between 1665 and 1690. This unusual, slow-moving bird was three feet tall and weighed about forty pounds. It seems to have remained only on its home island, 500 miles east of Madagascar in the Indian Ocean. The dodo had no natural enemies aside from sailors who ate the bird and their dogs and pigs, which ate dodo eggs.

ACTIVITY

Look up a list of the animals scientists expect to be extinct soon. Choose one and write a defense of it, explaining why it should be protected. Suggest things that young people like you can do to help save the animal you have chosen.

Prayer

People of the seventeenth century were game changers, dear Lord. They were religious leaders, explorers, artists, writers, pilgrims, scientists, and inventors. I too can be a game changer among my friends and classmates. Give me the grace to see when I should say a good word or approach a person in need. Help me make a difference in the lives of others.
Amen.

The Bigger Picture

Advances in mathematics and science were made during this century. Everything from calculators to thermometers to "water closets" (better known as toilets) became part of daily life. Great intellectual discoveries were made, too. In 1651 an Italian astronomer named Giovanni Riccioli made a map of the moon. And Isaac Newton discovered his famous law of gravity and laws of motion in 1666.

Many great books were written at this time, but the greatest may have been the publication in English of the King James Bible in 1611. This translation of Sacred Scripture made God's word more accessible to common people. Also during this period, two Church practices that had been used to justify the Protestant Reformation were ended. Nepotism and simony were officially prohibited by Pope Innocent XII in 1691.

Despite these positive steps, the Church continued to fragment into more and more Protestant denominations. The human family also continued to find reasons to war against one another. We will see this sad state of affairs continue over the next three centuries.

Chapter 18

1706—Benjamin Franklin is born.

AD 1710

1714—D.G. Fahrenheit invents the mercury thermometer.

1716—Spain establishes four missions in Texas.

AD 1720

AD 1730

1738—Excavation begins on Herculaneum, an Italian city buried
 beneath volcanic ash with the city of Pompeii.

1739—John Wesley begins the Methodist Church.

1740–1758—Pope Benedict XIV appoints first women as professors
 to papal universities in Bologna and reforms canonization procedures.
 He is an intellectual open to all sciences.

AD 1740

1741—Vitus Bering discovers the passageway between Russia and Alaska,
 now called the Bering Strait.

AD 1750

AD 1760

1762—Catherine the Great rules until her death in 1796. She is Russia's
 longest-reigning female ruler.

AD 1770

AD 1780

1791—The slave rebellion in Haiti, led by Toussaint L'Ouverture,
 frees the slaves and wins independence from France.

AD 1790

Foundations and Revolutions

In the eighteenth century new ideas began to take root in different parts of the world. The winds of knowledge and change were blowing everywhere. We will see this especially with the founding of the United States of America.

18th century

Jesuit astronomers with Emperor Kangxi

Outlawed in China

In 1715 Pope Clement XI wrote to all Catholic missionaries in China and India. He told them that the cultures and customs of local peoples could not be reflected in the Mass. For the sake of unity everything was to be done as it was in the West. The Church would later regret that decision. The ban on inculturation (adding local culture) was not reversed until Pius XII became pope in 1939. In the meantime, China outlawed Christian teaching in 1716. And by 1721, the Chinese emperor prohibited Christian missions in China.

Jansenism

Heresies seem to be part of every era, and this century was no exception. A Catholic movement known as Jansenism took hold in France. In 1713, it was condemned by Pope Clement XI. Jansenism denied that we have free will. Instead, Jansenists taught that God creates each one of us as either good or bad; nothing we do, Jansenists taught, can change this. They said that God's grace was ineffective for some people and could not be resisted for others. They believed that if you could live by a very strict moral code, it meant that you were saved. That is why many Jansenists became scrupulous (SKREW-pew-luhs); they constantly worried about being perfect. It is also why they tended to be very judgmental of others. Jansenists distorted Christianity in essentially the same way Calvin had during the Protestant Reformation. The main difference was that Jansenists chose to remain within the Church.

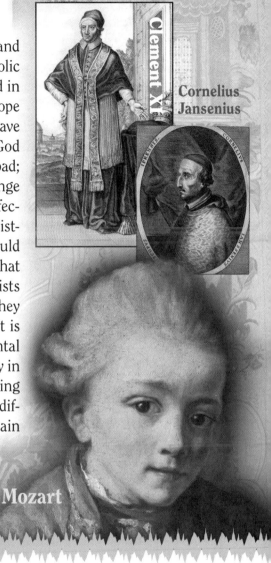

Clement XI

Cornelius Jansenius

Mozart

"Hello! My name is Ava. Last night my parents took me to a concert. You will never guess who the principal musician was! It was an eight-year-old boy named Wolfgang Amadeus Mozart. He composed a whole symphony by himself. Isn't that amazing? It was very impressive and beautiful. Perhaps he will become a famous composer when he grows up."

I Witness

The Awakening

Meanwhile, in the colonies of America, a new religious movement was beginning among the Protestants. It was known as the Great Awakening. The earlier form of worship the Puritans had introduced was not inspiring people's faith; it was too reserved and unemotional. Many Protestant denominations were now moved by lively preachers and frequent spiritual rallies. They began to display a more open and enthusiastic commitment to faith.

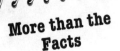

Mystery of History

There is a strange inscription on the Shugborough monument in Staffordshire, England. Does it reveal the location of the Holy Grail? Legend says the Grail—the cup used by Jesus at the Last Supper—was left in England (or Scotland) by the Knights Templar in the eighteenth century.

More than the Facts

The first piano was made in 1704 in Florence, Italy. It was created by a harpsichord maker, Bartolomeo Cristofori, and had a four-octave range. It was called a pianoforte because it could be played both softly and loudly. (In Italian, *piano* means soft and *forte* means loud.)

New France

By the beginning of the eighteenth century, North American territory belonging to France was at its largest. But the population of New France remained small; British American colonies were home to twenty times more people.

Thanks to the French, several important American cities were founded. These include Detroit in 1701, New Orleans in 1718, and Baton Rouge in 1719. By 1753, settlers in covered wagons began to trek across the vast plains. They and their families were in search of new farmland.

The Seven Years' War (1756–1763) between France and England was fought all over the world. (In North America it is also known as the French and Indian War.) When Britain gained final victory, the political power of France in the present day United States came to an end. French territories were surrendered to Great Britain in 1763. What remained would be sold to the United States in the Louisiana Purchase of 1803. Still, the culture and Catholic faith of the French inhabitants was preserved. That faith and culture live on today, both in Canada and the United States.

LATEST & GREATEST

The sandwich was created by John Montagu, Earl of Sandwich, in 1762. He had an idea for a snack that could be conveniently eaten anywhere. He got the idea one day when he was hungry while playing the gaming tables in London. The first sandwiches were meat and cheese between slices of bread.

The American Revolution

By the middle of the century, the colonies' discontent with British rule had come to a head. In places like Massachusetts Bay, Virginia, and South Carolina, there was a growing desire to break away from England. This desire led to the American Revolution, fought from 1775 to 1783. The Declaration of Independence, which proclaimed the colonies independent of Britain, was adopted on July 4, 1776. And in 1787 the constitution that formed the United States of America was written. We may already be familiar with names such as Washington, Jefferson, Adams, and Revere. Catholics made important contributions, too. The influence of Catholic patriots is noteworthy, since they only made up 1.5 percent of the population that fought for independence. The following are a few of these heroic men:

★ Commodore John Barry (1745–1803) was the son of an Irish tenant farmer. He became a ship's master in Philadelphia. Barry is often called the "father of the U.S. Navy," because he readied the first vessels as warships and successfully commanded them in battle.

★ Commodore Joshua Barney (1759–1818) was a native of Baltimore. He began his sailing career at age thirteen. A series of unforeseen events left him in command of a ship at fourteen! Barney went on to become a hero in the Continental Navy. He was the youngest naval commander in the Revolutionary War.

★ Marie-Joseph Paul Yves Roch Gilbert du Motier, Marquis de Lafayette (1757–1834), was born and trained in France. Lafayette volunteered to assist the Continental Army. He was especially instrumental in battles such as Yorktown.

★ Louis Lebègue Duportail (1743–1802) was a French military leader. He volunteered to act as chief engineer during the Revolutionary War. Duportail rose to the rank of colonel.

★ General Casimir Pulaski (1745–1779) was a Polish military officer. He volunteered to fight in the Revolutionary War. Pulaski died during the siege of Savannah, Georgia. He is known as the "father of the American cavalry."

★ Captain Thomas Fitzsimons (1741–1811) was a merchant and statesman. During the revolution he led a battalion from Pennsylvania. Fitzsimons represented Pennsylvania at the Continental Congress and the Constitutional Convention. He was one of only two Catholic signers of the U.S. Constitution; the other was Daniel Carroll of Maryland.

★ Colonel John Fitzgerald (d. 1799) was a native of Ireland. He owned a business in Philadelphia but joined Washington as his trusted aide and private secretary. The two remained good friends after the war. Both played a part in the founding of St. Mary's Catholic Church in Alexandria, Virginia in 1795 (before that, Catholic liturgies had been held in Colonel Fitzgerald's home).

★ Daniel Carroll (1730–1796) was the older brother of the first U.S. Catholic bishop. In 1778 he had the honor of signing both the original declaration to form a union of thirteen colonies and the Articles of Confederation and Perpetual Union. Later, in 1787, he signed the Constitution of the United States. His cousin, Charles Carroll (1737–1832), was the only Catholic to sign the Declaration of Independence (1776).

On the Record

General George Washington personally thanked Catholics who took part in the American Revolution. The following words are taken from a letter he wrote to Charles and John Carroll. It is dated March 15, 1790.

"As mankind becomes more liberal they will be more apt to allow that all those who conduct themselves as worthy members of the community are equally entitled to the protection of civil government. I hope ever to see America among the foremost nations in examples of justice and liberality. And I presume that your fellow-citizens will not forget the patriotic part which you took in the accomplishment of their Revolution and the establishment of their government; or the important assistance which they received from a nation in which the Roman Catholic faith is professed."

Bishop John Carroll

On the advice of Benjamin Franklin, Pope Pius VI chose a leader for the Catholic Church in America. John Carroll (1735–1815) was appointed "Superior of the Missions in the Thirteen States of North America" in 1784. Now the U.S. Church could begin to organize.

In 1790 John Carroll was consecrated bishop of Baltimore. He was the first and only Catholic bishop in the United States at this time. Carroll's task was to lead all the Catholics in the new nation. One of the first things the new bishop did was to call together his priests in 1791 for the first Synod of Baltimore. In the same year, Bishop Carroll helped to establish Georgetown University under the direction of the Jesuits. He also asked priests of the Company of Saint Sulpice to open St. Mary's College and Seminary in Baltimore. And he brought the Visitation nuns and the Discalced Carmelites to Maryland.

Pius VI

Benjamin Franklin

John Carroll

Mission San Diego

Junípero Serra

Saint Junípero Serra

Other parts of the vast North American continent were changing in the eighteenth century. Although the Spanish had discovered California in 1542, they had not established colonies. That changed in 1769 with the arrival of Saint Junípero Serra (1713–1784) and his fellow Franciscan friars. Together they opened Mission San Diego de Alcalá. It was the first of a string of twenty-one Spanish missions in California. The Franciscans brought many Native Peoples to faith in Christ. Unfortunately, the missions also brought them under Spanish rule, which at times was unjust to them. To maintain control of the area known to the Spanish as Alta California, four military *presidios*, or forts, were set up, one each in San Diego, Santa Barbara, Monterey, and San Francisco.

SNAPSHOT

Pierre Toussaint

Pierre Toussaint (1766–1853) was born a slave in Saint-Domingue (present-day Haiti). He emigrated to New York in 1787 with the Bérards, his master's family. Monsieur Bérard taught Pierre to read and apprenticed him to a hairdresser. When his master died unexpectedly, Pierre financially supported his master's wife and household. Few people ever knew that her bills were being paid by her Haitian servant. Before Madame Bérard's own death, she granted Pierre his freedom.

He married a woman named Juliette whose freedom he had paid for earlier. They never had children, but together they raised his niece and cared for a number of orphans. Pierre was a very generous man. He supported several charities and served the poor, the sick, and the dying all around the city. Devoted to prayer and works of charity, Pierre Toussaint is buried below the main altar of St. Patrick's Cathedral in New York City. He was declared Venerable in 1996 by Pope John Paul II.

Spinoza

Descartes

Louis XIV

Voltaire

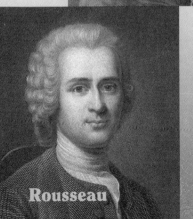

Rousseau

The Enlightenment

The second revolution of the century took place in France. We might say it began the century before, with the writings of philosophers such as René Descartes (1596–1650) and Baruch Spinoza (1632–1677). Both of these men sought to replace faith with human reasoning.

This new movement was called rationalism. It discouraged belief in God as Father, Son, and Holy Spirit and promoted deism, which is belief in God as a faraway, impersonal power. Deists do not believe in revelation; therefore they do not see the Bible as God's word. Things got worse when the French king, Louis XIV, died in 1715 and a French philosopher known as Voltaire (1694–1778) became popular. He was a sworn enemy of the Catholic Church and intended to wipe it out.

Jean-Jacques Rousseau (1712–1778) was another famous thinker of the time. He spearheaded a writing project called the *Encyclopedie*. This was a large series of books with many contributors. They presented knowledge from the viewpoint of reason with no reference to faith.

These free-thinking philosophies came to be known as the Enlightenment.

Jesuits Banned

The wave against religious faith may have been the biggest force behind the banning of the Society of Jesus throughout Europe. The Jesuits were an international order with strong ties to the pope. Leaders of nations saw them as a serious threat and wanted to limit their influence. In the middle of the eighteenth century, European nations expelled Jesuits from their countries. Because the Society of Jesus could no longer accomplish its mission, Pope Clement XIV suppressed the order in 1773. It wasn't until 1815 that the Jesuits were restored to full service within the Church. This was possible because civil governments in Europe became more stable again after the final defeat of Napoleon.

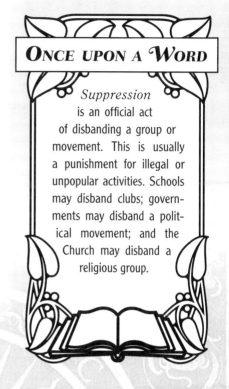

ONCE UPON A WORD

Suppression is an official act of disbanding a group or movement. This is usually a punishment for illegal or unpopular activities. Schools may disband clubs; governments may disband a political movement; and the Church may disband a religious group.

Jesuit priest in Brazil

The French Revolution

People across Europe were inspired by the success of the American Revolution. Meanwhile, discontent grew over those from the rich upper classes who lived privileged lives. Members of the royalty were especially unpopular. They claimed a "divine right of kings," which made a monarch's word law. The common people grew increasingly frustrated over the way they were being treated.

On July 14, 1789 a crowd attacked the Parisian prison known as the Bastille. This event marked the start of the French Revolution. Although the revolutionaries proclaimed they were for "liberty, equality, and fraternity," the revolution became just a reverse of power. Members of the ruling class, priests, and religious were arrested and killed. Property was confiscated. As so often happens in revolutions, the stolen property didn't go to help the poor. Instead, it was used to enrich leaders of the revolt. Churches were desecrated. Great cathedrals like Notre Dame in Paris were used to worship human reason rather than God. Many great works of art were destroyed. For a time, statues of the Virgin Mary were replaced by images of "Lady Liberty."

King Louis XVI and his family were executed in 1793. This horribly violent time is called the Reign of Terror. People of faith were not safe. Eventually, the revolutionists began fighting one another; they destroyed the ideals of liberty, equality, and brotherhood they had promised to bring. This is where Napoleon Bonaparte appears in history. He restored order to France but was an ambitious man who hoped to make himself the next great emperor of Europe.

ACTIVITY

If you were going to start missions today like the California missions founded by Saint Junípero Serra (1769), where would you do it? Find out about an area in your country that needs churches. What would you plan for that area?

Prayer

Dear God, help me to appreciate the good things done by others. If I am able to do so, let me assist them to do good. Help me to stay true to my faith, even in difficult times or when it is not popular to do so. When I see someone in trouble or in need, show me how to help by informing my parents, teachers, or others about what I see. By doing good and caring for those in need, I know I am helping your Church to grow. Amen.

The Bigger Picture

Led by Napoleon, the French army defeated papal troops in 1796 and entered Rome. They demanded that Pope Pius VI (1717–1799), who had condemned the French Revolution, officially recognize the new political order in France. Pius made some concessions. Shortly after, when a French general was murdered in Rome, the army proclaimed a new Roman Republic. The pope was arrested and the Papal States were taken. Pius VI died while imprisoned in the French city of Valence. The Church's enemies thought the papacy had finally ended, but Pope Pius VI had wisely arranged for the next conclave. The nineteenth century would see a resurgence of the influence of the papacy.

Many challenges faced the Church. She tried to meet not only the needs of people from newly discovered lands, but also of the many emigrants to these places. Another type of revolution would soon begin, which we know as the Industrial Revolution. An era of progress was coming. Machines would begin to accomplish numberless tasks previously done by hand laborers. The Church would now have to reflect on how the teachings of Jesus could speak to new situations being created by social progress. Papal teachings would focus on the development of peoples and on issues of social justice.

Chapter 19

1804—Meriwether Lewis and William Clark, along with Sacajawea, their Native American guide, begin to explore territory across North America to the Pacific.

AD 1810

1812—Napoleon's army attacks Russia but retreats, with only one-sixth of his troops surviving the harsh winter.

1818—The Zulu Empire is founded by Chaka in southern Africa.

AD 1820

AD 1830

1836—Texas wins independence from Mexico.
1837—Victoria becomes Queen of England.
1840—Upper and Lower Canada are united by the Union Act.

AD 1840

1848—The Communist Manifesto is written by German socialists Karl Marx and Friedrich Engels.

AD 1850

AD 1860

1863—Lincoln writes the Emancipation Proclamation freeing the slaves in the United States.
1867—Canadian Confederation—the process by which British Canadian colonies were united into one Dominion of Canada—takes place.
1869—The Suez Canal opens in Egypt.

AD 1870

1876—The Battle of Little Bighorn, Custer's last stand against the Lakota (Sioux) and other tribes of the Great Plains, takes place.

AD 1880

AD 1890

1900—The Boxer Rebellion in China targets foreigners.

A Time of Progress

19th century

Medical Advances

Many of the most important health discoveries were made in the nineteenth century. For instance, the process of purifying milk was developed in 1864. It was named pasteurization in honor of Louis Pasteur, the scientist who discovered it. In 1880 Pasteur also developed the principle of vaccination.

One of the most interesting persons in the medical field was Mary Ann (Ball) Bickerdyke (1817–1901). Before her marriage she studied herbal medicine at Ohio's Oberlin College. She and her husband moved to Galesburg, Illinois, where they raised two sons. During the American Civil War in 1861, Mary Ann was sent to deliver medical supplies to the Union army in a nearby town. When she saw the terrible condition of the camp hospital, she stayed to clean it. She became an agent of the U.S. Sanitary Commission. Mary Ann is recognized for setting a standard of care that is reflected in hospitals even today. Together with a dedicated core of nurses, "Mother" Bickerdyke established 300 field hospitals. She cared for wounded soldiers on nineteen battlefields.

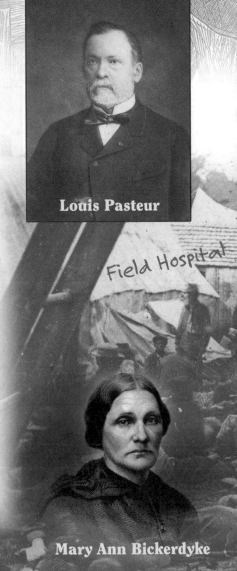

Louis Pasteur

Field Hospital

Mary Ann Bickerdyke

LATEST & GREATEST

Alfred Nobel (1833–1896) is best known today as the founder of the prestigious Nobel Prizes. They are given annually to persons who have excelled in science, literature, or the pursuit of peace. Nobel was born in Sweden. He himself was a chemist, an engineer, an industrialist, and a writer. His greatest scientific accomplishment was the development of dynamite. Nobel's invention became one of the greatest assets for mining, for construction, and for opening up routes for travel. Unfortunately, it also led to the development of many deadly weapons for war. It is thought that Nobel established his prizes as a way to make up for the destructive power of his principal invention.

SNAPSHOT

Gregor Mendel

Gregor Johann Mendel (1822–1884) was born in the empire of Austria-Hungary. He became an Augustinian priest and was sent to study philosophy and physics. As a teacher he began to experiment with pea plants and bees. Before Mendel, scientists believed that traits were passed down equally from parent plants. Mendel discovered that some traits are more likely to be expressed in future generations; these he called "dominant." Other traits hide and may not show up for several generations. He called these "recessive." Mendel's work was not fully appreciated until after his death. Other scientists studying inherited traits came upon Mendel's papers and realized that his theories verified their findings. Today, he is recognized as the father of genetics.

Napoleon

Wilhelm

Victoria

Napoleon Bonaparte

Napoleon Bonaparte (1769–1821) played a starring role at the start of this century. He was a great military commander who managed to end the Holy Roman Empire and make himself emperor over most of Europe. In 1801 he formulated a concordat (agreement) with the Catholic Church. The agreement restored the Church's position in France while it allowed Napoleon to control Church finances and the appointment of the bishops. He also created a code of law giving citizens a degree of freedom and equality they had not known before. Napoleon was finally defeated in 1815 at the famous Battle of Waterloo in what is now Belgium. He was exiled to an island in the Mediterranean, where he died.

Nations and Empires

Napoleon wasn't the only emperor of this century. Various regions were unified that had been under the rule of dukes or princes for many centuries before. Italy made Rome its capital in 1871. That same year, most of the Protestant German lands united under Kaiser (German for Caesar) Wilhelm. Traditionally Catholic Austria and Hungary formed the Austro-Hungarian Empire in 1867. Russia had extended its borders and could also claim "empire" status. It was ruled by a czar (Russian for Caesar). Stung by its loss of the American colonies, Great Britain built a powerful navy and established thriving colonies on every continent. During the reign of Queen Victoria, it was said that the "sun never set on the British Empire." The United States continued to extend westward to the Pacific Ocean. Japanese and Chinese empires competed for power and trade in the Far East. The Ottoman Empire, though in decline, still ruled Greece, Asia Minor, and parts of North Africa under a sultan.

Political Sources of Restoration for the Church

The new century seemed to be a time of restoration for the Church. In 1829, the Catholic Emancipation Act was passed in England. It allowed Catholics once more to hold public office. In 1850, the Catholic Church was permitted to reestablish bishops and thirteen dioceses in the United Kingdom. Meanwhile in Spain, the Spanish Inquisition was officially closed.

Adding to this time of change for the Church was the election of Pope Blessed Pius IX. He was the longest-reigning pope in history after Saint Peter. Though he suffered from epilepsy, Pius IX served thirty-one years, from 1846 to 1878. Pope Pius IX ruled the Papal States with a spirit of reform. Soon, however, the Papal States were swallowed up by various rulers competing for supreme power in Italy. When Victor Emmanuel conquered Rome in 1861, the papacy was left with just a tiny city-state we know as Vatican City. The worldly power of the popes was over. It didn't take long for the Church to understand that this was liberating. Now the popes could concentrate all of their attention on the spiritual state of the Church.

Victor

Pius IX

ITALY (Rome)

city wall

Vatican Museums

Saint Peter's Basilica

Saint Peter's Square

0   0.15   0.3 km
0   0.15   0.3 mi

ITALY (Rome)

The First Vatican Council

Pope Pius IX called for the First Ecumenical Vatican Council—that is, the first worldwide council—to be held in Rome from 1869 to 1870. This was the first church council since Trent in the sixteenth century! An important thing that came out of this council was our understanding of the authority of the pope. The council declared that the pope was first among the bishops. It also proclaimed that the Holy Spirit would not allow the pope or the bishops gathered together in council to teach errors about faith or morals. This is known as infallibility.

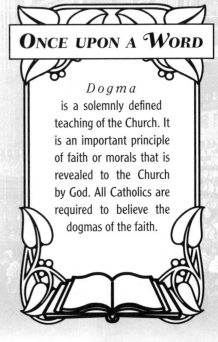

ONCE UPON A WORD

Dogma is a solemnly defined teaching of the Church. It is an important principle of faith or morals that is revealed to the Church by God. All Catholics are required to believe the dogmas of the faith.

Mystery of History

There is a mysterious linen cloth believed to be the burial cloth of Jesus. Today it is enshrined in the Cathedral of St. John the Baptist in Turin, Italy. This relic is known as the Shroud of Turin. The cloth measures approximately 13½ feet long by 4½ feet wide. It bears the image of man lying down. Its origins are unknown, and how it came to the West in the fourteenth century is also unclear. But the shroud has been publicly venerated in Turin since 1578.

In 1898 a photographer named Secondo Pia took the first photographs of the shroud. While doing so, he made an astonishing discovery. The shroud's image is actually a photographic negative. That is, the dark parts of the image are shown as light, and the light areas are dark. How could that be possible centuries before photography was invented? Why would someone painting a forgery make the image a negative? Could the glorious light of the Resurrection have created the impression?

Leo XIII

The Industrial Revolution

The Industrial Revolution spanned the mid-eighteenth to mid-nineteenth centuries. New sources of power and machines were developed. There were also better forms of transportation for raw materials and finished products. As a result, a revolution began in all areas of manufacturing. For owners and managers it was a time of prosperity. For others, including many children, it was a difficult time marked by long work hours, poor conditions, health hazards, and little financial benefit. Laws limiting child labor were not passed until much later.

In response to such obvious inequality, the next pope, Leo XIII (1810–1903), addressed these issues in writing. In 1891 he issued the encyclical *Rerum Novarum* or "On Capital and Labor." This encyclical would become the model for all Church teachings on how to live and work together in justice and peace. Pope Leo recognized the dangers of communism and socialism. These new political and economic ideas sought solutions to injustices, but they were harmful in other ways. Pope Leo issued warnings about them to the whole Church.

Changing Borders

Other areas of the Catholic world were changing. France misjudged the future value of the Louisiana territories and sold them to the United States in 1803. The following year, Haiti won independence from France. In 1819 Simón Bolívar liberated a large area of South America from Spain. Ten years later, his Greater Colombia became the countries we know today as Colombia, Ecuador, Venezuela, and Panama. In 1821, Spanish rule of Mexico ended. The following year, Brazil declared itself independent of Portugal. Fourteen years later, Texas gained independence from Mexico. And the border between Canada and the United States was decided upon in 1842.

Simón Bolívar

Elizabeth Ann Seton

Saint Elizabeth Ann Seton

Born in New York, Elizabeth Ann Seton (1774–1821) was a widow and convert to Catholicism. In 1808 she went to Baltimore to set up a school for girls. The archbishop of Baltimore, John Carroll, gave Elizabeth great encouragement and support. A year later, she and her companions began a new religious community. They called themselves the Sisters of Charity, and Elizabeth became known as Mother Seton. The sisters opened schools and orphanages all over the East Coast. In fact, Mother Seton is credited with founding the Catholic school system in the United States. She died in 1821 and was buried in Emmitsburg, Maryland. There a shrine has been established in her honor. Mother Seton was canonized in 1975. She is the first native-born citizen of the United States to be named a saint.

Migration and the American Civil War

In the first half of the nineteenth century, European Catholics began to arrive in North America in great numbers. More than one million Irish Catholics migrated to the United States and Canada. Many came because of the potato famine in Ireland (1845–1849), which claimed a million lives. The gold rushes—1848 in California, U.S. and 1896 in Yukon, Canada—brought large numbers of prospectors in search of fortune. There were entire "Irish brigades" that served in the armies on both sides of the Civil War. Many Irish also went to work building the transcontinental railway.

Catholic immigration meant challenge and growth for the Catholic Church in North America. Those who came were often poor farmworkers. Sometimes they had little knowledge of English. These were courageous and hardworking people. They were willing to do whatever was necessary to begin new lives in the new world.

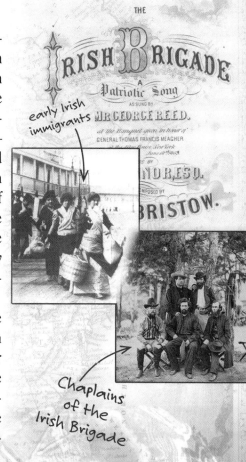

early Irish immigrants

Chaplains of the Irish Brigade

"Hello. I am called Sophie by my teachers, although at home I have another name. We are *Potawotomi*, which means 'keepers of the fire.' I think our language is difficult for the sisters to learn. Some who are younger speak it well enough to teach us. They are also very kind. My favorite sister is the oldest one. Her name is Mother Rose Philippine Duchesne, but we call her *Quahkahkanumad*. It means 'woman who always prays.' She cannot speak our language, but she smiles at us and shows us her praying hands."

I Witness

On the Record

Chief Joseph (1840–1904) was the son of a chief who had been one of the first members of his tribe, the Nez Percé, to convert to the Catholic faith. Born Hin-mah-too-lat-kekt ("Thunder Traveling to the Loftier Mountain Heights") in Wallowa Valley, Oregon Territory, he was given the Christian name Joseph at Baptism.

In the late nineteenth century the Nez Percé people were forced to accept a treaty with white settlers. Some of the Native Americans revolted against the false promises that the settlers made. Several settlers were killed. Chief Joseph knew retribution would be harsh, so in 1877 he led his band of 700 toward safety in Canada. For four months the Nez Percé traveled across nearly 1,700 miles. The bitter winter and constant skirmishes with U.S. soldiers finally took a toll on them. With only eighty-seven warriors left, and starving women and children, he surrendered with these powerful words:

"Tell General Howard I know his heart. What he told me before I have in my heart. I am tired of fighting. Our Chiefs are killed; Looking Glass is dead, Ta Hool Hool Shute is dead. The old men are all dead. It is the young men who say yes or no. He who led the young men is dead. It is cold, and we have no blankets; the little children are freezing to death. My people, some of them, have run away to the hills, and have no blankets, no food. No one knows where they are—perhaps freezing to death. I want to have time to look for my children, and see how many of them I can find. Maybe I shall find them among the dead. Hear me, my Chiefs! I am tired; my heart is sick and sad. From where the sun now stands I will fight no more forever."

—Chief Joseph "Thunder Traveling to the Loftier Mountain Heights", 1877

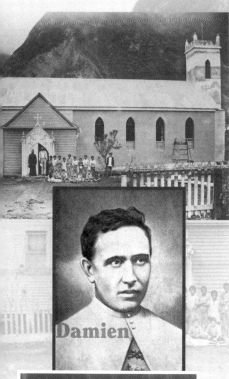

Damien

Katherine

Dominic

Saint Damien of Molokai

A young Belgian arrived in the Hawaiian Islands in 1864. He was a member of the Congregation of the Sacred Hearts of Jesus and Mary. Two months later, this man was ordained a Catholic priest. Father Jozef Damien de Veuster (1840–1889) left his home-land for a mission halfway across the globe. In 1873 he heroically volunteered to spend his most productive years as the priest of a leper colony on the island of Molokai. At the time there were at least 600 lepers of various faiths and some of no faith. Father Damien became father, carpenter, teacher, nurse, and friend to all. After sixteen years of selfless service, Damien himself contracted leprosy and died. He was canonized by Pope Benedict XVI in 2009.

Saints of the 19th Century

There are many other examples of holi-ness in the nineteenth century. Among them are Saint Katharine Drexel (1858–1955), a wealthy Philadelphia heiress who founded the Sisters of the Blessed Sacrament to serve American Indians and African Americans, as well as more than 200 schools and missions for their education; Saint Thérèse of Lisieux (1873–1897), the young French Carmelite patroness of the missions; Saint John Bosco (1815–1888), an Italian priest who ministered to boys living on the streets and founded the Salesians to give them job training as well as religious education; Saint Dominic Savio (1842–1857), a student of Saint John Bosco who intended to serve young people but died at fifteen; Blessed John Henry Newman (1801–1890), a priest in the Church of England who became one of the most influential converts of the century; and Saint Catherine Labouré (1806–1876), a Daughter of Charity in France, who encountered the Virgin Mary and gave the "Miraculous Medal" to the world. She kept her vision a secret all her life, and did not let anyone know the medal had come from her.

The Immaculate Conception

A crowning glory of this century came when Pope Pius IX declared the Dogma of the Immaculate Conception in 1854. For centuries, the Church had taught that God had created the Blessed Virgin Mary free from original sin. But the Holy Father wanted to proclaim this honor as an official teaching of the Catholic faith. In this way the Church would show its gratitude to Mary for her constant care. Four years later, in 1858, a young peasant girl named Bernadette Soubirous (1844–1879) was blessed with visions of Our Lady at Lourdes in southwestern France. There the Blessed Mother identified herself as "the Immaculate Conception."

John Henry

Catherine

Bernadette

Lourdes

Armand
David

Elaphurus
davidianus

More than the Facts

Father Armand David (1826–1900) was the first Westerner to see pandas. This priest was a French Vincentian missionary to China as well as a botanist and zoologist. He introduced gerbils to the West and helped save a species of deer from extinction. It was later named for him (*Elaphurus davidianus*). Father David brought back many well-documented samples for museums, including sixty-three new species of animals and 250 new species of plants.

ACTIVITY

Of all the famous people who lived in the nineteenth century, whom would you like to meet? Think of one question you would want to ask this person. What do you think that person would want to ask you?

Prayer

Dear God, in studying this century I have seen that your people are always making progress. Even your Church makes progress in understanding your truths and in holiness. Make me a pioneer in faith, one who is not afraid to cross into new ways of seeing things. Help me to be a person who always grows wiser and stronger. Make me also a little holier every day.

Amen.

The Bigger Picture

The discoveries and developments of the nineteenth century set the stage for a glorious twentieth century. That century would be full of progress and achievement. But a series of frightening and vicious wars would also show that true glory is found when the human spirit seeks the will of God.

At his Ascension our Lord directed the Church to go forth and make disciples of all nations. This may seem like an impossible task when we read about the suffering inflicted by one people upon another. As members of the Church of Jesus, however, it is our mission to try to bring every person to him. We can do this by sharing Jesus' Gospel message of peace with each person we meet, and by living the kindness of Christ.

As you read about the twentieth century, think of how things should have been. What could Christians have done to make God's Kingdom more visible here on earth?

Chapter 20

AD 1910

1912—The luxury cruise ship Titanic sinks with loss of over 1,500 lives.

AD 1920

1920—Women are allowed to vote in the United States; women in Canada are allowed to vote in 1921.

1926—The persecution of the Church in Mexico known as the Cristero War or La Cristiada begins.

AD 1930

1937—J.R.R. Tolkien's first fantasy novel, *The Hobbit*, is published. He publishes *Lord of the Rings* in three books in 1954 and 1955.

AD 1940

1945—The United Nations is formed.

1948—Israel is founded as a homeland for Jews.

AD 1950

1961—Russian Yuri Gagarin is the first man in space.

AD 1960

1965—The mutual excommunication from the Great Schism of 1054 against Catholic and Orthodox is lifted by both parties.

1967–St. Joseph's Oratory in Montreal is completed. It is the largest basilica dedicated to St. Joseph, Canada's patron, in the world.

AD 1970

1968—Martin Luther King, Jr., is assassinated.

1969—Neil Armstrong and Edwin Aldrin make a successful moon landing in Apollo 11.

AD 1980

1979—Mother Teresa of Calcutta wins the Nobel Peace Prize for her work with the poorest of the poor in the streets and slums of India.

1994—800,000 people are slaughtered in the Rwandan genocide.

AD 1990

1994—Nelson Mandela is elected president of South Africa.

War and Peace

The twentieth century seems to have been an age marked by warfare. Conflicts took place all over the world: the Chinese Revolution, the Mexican Revolution, the Russian Revolution, World Wars I and II, the Korean War, the Vietnam War, the Spanish Civil War, the Japanese/Chinese Civil War, the Israel/Palestinian War, and the Arab-Israeli War. These wars caused immense suffering. Societies and cultures were radically changed. Christians—and many other groups of people—were persecuted.

Your grandparents, and great-grandparents were born in this century. It was a time packed with amazing achievements as well as untold sufferings.

Science again brought great blessings to the world. In 1901 Marie Curie found out how to make use of radioactivity. In 1913 Henry Ford unveiled the assembly line; with it he could mass produce automobiles. In 1927 Charles Lindbergh was the first aviator to fly by himself across the Atlantic. In 1928 Alexander Fleming discovered penicillin. And in 1952 Jonas Salk developed a vaccine to prevent polio.

Great strides were also made in the world of communication. The telegraph gave way to the telephone. Radio, movies, television, and eventually the Internet made this age a time of increased communication.

20th century

Marie

Alexander

Ford's assembly line

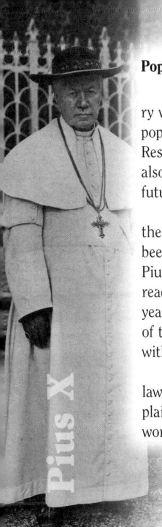

Pius X

Pope Saint Pius X

One of the greatest gifts to the Church in this century was Pope Saint Pius X (1835–1914). Elected in 1903, the pope took as his papal motto "to restore all things in Christ." Restoration was precisely what the Church needed; it was also what the whole world would need in the immediate future.

As pope, Pius X lowered the age for children to receive the Eucharist. In previous years, first Holy Communion had been given when children were twelve or fourteen years old. Pius changed this; children could now receive when they reached the "age of reason," usually when a child is seven years old. The pope encouraged children to treasure the gift of the Eucharist. He asked them to receive Jesus often and with the intention of bringing unbelievers to faith.

Pope Pius X did many other things. He reformed Church law, improved liturgical music, and made many efforts to explain the theological error of his day—Modernism. He also worked to help nations avoid conflict and war.

The World at War

Unfortunately, Pope Pius X died just as World War I began in 1914. Called the Great War, it was supposed to be "the war to end all wars." Recent advancements in technology and weapons caused World War I to be more destructive than any war before it had been. It lasted just over four years but cost millions of lives; nine million soldiers and seven million civilians were killed. In addition, the persecution of Armenian Christians in 1915 by the Ottoman government ended with some 1.5 million deaths.

World War I changed how Europeans saw themselves and the world. It also caused worldwide an unmatched wave of hopelessness and despair. The terrible losses from World War I are commemorated each year on November 11. This was the day the Treaty of Versailles was signed, ending the war. Canadians observe this event as Remembrance Day, and citizens of the United States as Veterans Day.

ONCE UPON A WORD

An *apparition* (ap-uh-RISH-uhn) is a vision of Jesus, the Virgin Mary, another saint, or an angel. The Church carefully investigates any claim that an apparition has taken place before approving it. A number of apparitions, however, are recognized as genuine. There are two very important appearances of Jesus: the Sacred Heart of Jesus to Saint Margaret Mary and the Divine Mercy to Saint Faustina. And some of the approved Marian apparitions include those at Lourdes, Fatima, and Guadalupe.

Our Lady of Fatima

During the anxiety and violence of this time, an incredible series of events took place. In 1917 the Blessed Virgin Mary appeared to three shepherd children. She would continue to visit them over the course of six months. These children were Lucia dos Santos and her cousins, Saints Francisco and Jacinta Marto. The visits or *apparitions* occurred in the Portuguese town of Fatima.

Our Lady of Fatima's message to the children was simple: make small sacrifices for the conversion of sinners and pray the rosary for peace. Tens of thousands of people witnessed the "Miracle of the Sun" at the final apparition. Millions were inspired to renew their faith. The two younger children died in a flu epidemic shortly after the apparitions ended. Lucia, however, grew up and became a Carmelite nun. She lived into her nineties, devoting her entire life to prayer and to living the message she had received.

A Fragile Peace

At the end of the war, a League of Nations was set up. Its mission was to help the transition to peace and to avoid future international conflicts. The league ultimately failed in this task, and the United Nations eventually took its place. World War I would lead to revolutions and new borders that would increase tension throughout Europe. In 1939 those tensions erupted in World War II.

The Great Depression and the Catholic Worker Movement

The Great Depression (1929–1941) was a time of severe hardship for many people. It caused a worldwide economic crisis. While a number of factors led to the depression, the most devastating was the crash of stock values on Wall Street in the United States in 1929. Because the stock market failed, investors lost great sums of money. Panicked people all over the world rushed to take their money out of the banks, which caused banks to crash as well. Suddenly, there was no money to buy goods or services. Without customers, companies went out of business. Millions of jobs were lost. Everyone seemed to be affected. Many people despaired; some even committed suicide since they could see no remedy.

In the midst of the Great Depression, God inspired people of faith to offer a Christian response. Dorothy Day (1897–1980) and Peter Maurin (1877–1949) were two such people. In 1933 they began the Catholic Worker Movement. Its aim was to give Gospel hope to millions of people out of work. The Catholic Worker Movement grew quickly. By 1936 there were thirty-three Hospitality Houses. They all offered shelter and community to the poor.

The Holocaust or *Shoah*

One of the worst crimes of the century came with the Nazi (National Socialist) Party's rise to power in Germany. Under the leadership of Adolf Hitler, the Nazis planned to create a "master race" of people. They began to eliminate people they labeled less valuable: Jews, mentally and physically disabled persons, and other groups. Death camps were set up in Germany, Poland, and other areas under Nazi control. Special units of the armed forces sought out the unwanted persons. They were then either herded into gas chambers or worked to death. Six million Jews and six million others were killed. We call this terrible crime the Holocaust, a word that means "burnt sacrifice," or *Shoah*, the Hebrew word for "great tragedy."

Many people found it hard to believe that something so horrible could really be happening. The depth of this tragedy was seen only when World War II ended. Troops were sent to liberate those being held in concentration camps. Very few of the prisoners survived. Those who had were suffering from abuse, extreme starvation, and disease.

The pope at the time, Pius XII (1876–1958), had told all convents, monasteries, and even the Vatican itself to shelter anyone seeking asylum. A number of heroic individuals joined in the fate of these poor victims. Among them were Catholic priests, religious, and laypeople.

members of the Canadian Royal 22e Regiment in audience with Pope Pius XII

Mystery of History

How could a man as evil as Adolf Hitler fool an entire nation? It seems impossible that a whole country could be unaware of the horrors in the concentration camps. How many other cruel injustices took place in this century? Why do people not notice when others are treated unfairly, even when it happens on such a large scale?

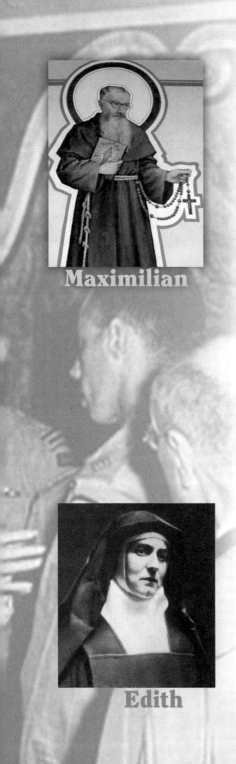

Maximilian

Edith

Saint Maximilian Kolbe

Saint Maximilian Kolbe was a Polish Franciscan friar (1894–1941). Father Kolbe published a Catholic newspaper. He was also known to oppose the Nazis. Because of these things, the friar was sent to the concentration camp at Auschwitz. While there, Father Kolbe volunteered to take the place of another prisoner sentenced to death. He did this because the condemned man had a wife and family. His request was granted. Father Maximilian remained alive in a starvation bunker for two weeks. He was finally executed by guards. The prisoner whose place he took survived the war and returned to his family.

Saint Edith Stein

Saint Edith Stein (1891–1942) was a Carmelite nun and philosopher. As an adult she had converted to the Catholic faith from Judaism. In 1933 Edith wrote to Pope Pius XI asking him to issue a papal statement against Hitler. The Holy Father wrote an encyclical against National Socialism (Nazism), but it had no effect against the Nazis. Next the Dutch bishops came out with a strong anti-Nazi statement. The Nazis responded by rounding up and executing religious and priests who were Jewish converts. Among them were Edith and her sister, who was also a convert to Catholicism.

Resistance

Many laypeople of deep Christian faith—Catholics, Protestants, and Orthodox—resisted Nazism and war. One of these was a young Catholic husband and father, Blessed Franz Jägerstätter (1907–1943). Franz was drafted into the Nazis but refused to serve or even put on a uniform; to him the regime represented pure evil. Franz Jägerstätter ended up being executed for his views.

In Holland, the ten Boom family did what they could to help. They courageously hid Jews in their home and assisted them in escaping persecution. The ten Boom sisters and father were discovered and sent to a concentration camp.

In Bulgaria the common people, intellectual leaders, king, and Orthodox Church all banded together. They worked to save 50,000 Jews who lived in Bulgaria from being sent to Nazi death camps.

Examples of Holiness

In times of great tragedy and evil God always provides shining examples of holiness. His goodness shines in ordinary people and in the extraordinary witness of his saints.

Many faith-filled people lived in the twentieth century. A great many have already been beatified or canonized. A few are mentioned in this chapter, but there are many more to learn about. These include Saint Faustina Kowalska (1905–1938), Saint Andre Bessette (1845–1937), Saint Josemaría Escrivá (1902–1975), Blessed James Alberione (1884–1971), Saint Mary MacKillop (1842–1909), Saint Padre Pio (1887–1968), Saint Mother Teresa of Calcutta (1910–1997), and Pope Saint John Paul II (1920–2005).

The Assumption

In 1950 Pope Pius XII, who had brought the Church through World War II, proclaimed another Marian dogma: the Assumption. It is celebrated by the whole Church every year on August 15. The Assumption of Mary is the Catholic belief that the Mother of Jesus was brought to heaven in her body as well as in her soul. There she shares fully in the resurrection of her Son.

"Did you hear the amazing news? Just when this Holy Year of 1950 is ending, our Holy Father Pope Pius XII made a special Christmas announcement. Archaeologists have found the tomb of Saint Peter! Oh, I'm Angelina, and when I grow up I want to be an archaeologist too. Anyway, the tomb has been under the altar in the Basilica of St. Peter all these centuries—just waiting to be discovered. And the really exciting thing is that the excavations are going to continue. Who knows what else archaeologists might find?"

I Witness

Communism

Between the beginning of World War I and the end of World War II, Communism grew. It gained strength and began to spread throughout the world. While Communism may have promised an end to poverty and injustice, Communist governments did just the opposite. In Communist countries, people were deprived of their human rights and freedom. An example of this was the manmade Ukrainian famine of 1932 and 1933. Between 2.5 and 7.5 million Ukrainians starved to death as part of a Soviet plan to end hopes for Ukrainian independence.

Communism suppressed the Church and other religions, while it actively promoted atheism. Christians in Communist countries were forced to practice their faith in secret. Many who were found out were imprisoned in labor camps; some simply disappeared.

Communists seized power in large nations like Russia (which was renamed the Union of Soviet Socialist Republic or U.S.S.R.) and China. Smaller countries like Albania, Cuba, Vietnam, and North Korea were often used as political colonies by the larger powers. By the 1960s, the U.S.S.R. controlled almost all of Eastern Europe and most of Central Asia. The People's Republic of China controlled much of Southeast Asia.

The Second Vatican Council and the Catechism

Meanwhile, the most important event of the twentieth century for the Church was unfolding. Pope Saint John XXIII opened the Second Ecumenical Vatican Council on October 11, 1962; it closed on December 8, 1965. So many advancements and changes in society had taken place. Pope John wanted his council to take up pastoral topics such as ecumenism, the liturgy, and the universal call to holiness. These issues, plus many others, were discussed by the bishops gathered in Rome. Sixteen documents were issued from Vatican II. They offered direction and inspiration for the Church to face her future with renewed understanding and confidence in the Holy Spirit's guidance. Many people remember Vatican II for its decision to allow the Mass to be celebrated in every language, rather than in Latin only.

In 1992 Pope John Paul II presented the Church with the *Catechism of the Catholic Church*. The new catechism was a wonderful source of instruction. It had been more than four hundred years since the whole Church had compiled a complete catechism. The *CCC*, as it is often called, offers a clear and compelling statement of faith under four headings: creed, sacraments, moral teachings, and prayer.

More than the Facts

There were three popes in one year. It was the year 1978. Blessed Pope Paul VI was elected on June 23, 1963 and died August 6, 1978. Next Pope John Paul I was elected August 26, 1978; he died thirty-three days later on September 28. Then Saint Pope John Paul II was elected October 16, 1978; he reigned until his death in 2005.

Protecting Human Life

The century was filled with power struggles and wars. It proved difficult for world nations to keep sight of the dignity of every person and the value of human life. Perhaps that is why another great sadness left its mark on this century: the scourge of legalized abortion.

Abortion is the killing of an unborn child while that child is developing inside its mother's womb. Abortion was first legalized in Canada in 1969. On January 23, 1973 the Supreme Court of the United States also made it lawful for a woman to abort an unborn child. Many other countries have done the same.

On the Record

It was July 20, 1969. American astronaut Neil Armstrong (1930–2012) stepped down from the Apollo 11 spacecraft onto the surface of the moon. As he did so, he made a statement that was heard around the world: "That's one small step for (a) man, one giant leap for mankind." In the next three years five more successful moon landings took place.

"Man was given an inquisitive nature, and that manifests itself in our desire to take that next step, to seek out the next great adventure. Going to the moon wasn't really a question, it was the next step in the evolution of our knowledge, of our understanding. It was necessary to explore the limits of our technology and set the stage for what mankind could achieve in the future."

—from *The Top Ten Phrases from the First Man on the Moon* by John P. Millis, Ph.D., Space/Astronomy Expert

Some two billion unborn children have been aborted around the world in less than fifty years. Just as the Church has always spoken out against errors in faith, she has also defended the value of every human life from conception until natural death. Thousands of people, many of them young persons, join the March for Life every year in Canada, the United States, and many other countries around the world. They do this to commemorate the day abortion was legalized. They also pray for law makers and for all who have had or who have performed abortions.

LATEST & GREATEST

Believe it or not, there was a world before personal computers. It might be hard to imagine such a pre-computer time. These were the days of handwritten letters and school assignments, trips to the library to do class reports, listening to music on phonographs, relying on newspapers for the latest stories, only three or four television channels, or waiting for the weekend to see a movie. Of course, computers have existed since the 1940s. They were complex systems used mainly by government agencies back then. And they were large enough to take up entire rooms! Personal computers first appeared in 1976. Immediately the race began to make them smaller, more powerful, and less expensive. Mathematical languages were developed; they allowed computers to perform many more intricate tasks and to connect in a world-spanning web. Personal computers became platforms for various activities. Today they are used for interactive games, publishing, entertainment, wartime combat strategies, shopping, stock trading, texting, and keeping in touch with Grandma.

XIII V MCMLXXXI

Threat to the Pope

In 1981, Ali Agca, a young Turkish assassin, tried to kill Pope John Paul II in St. Peter's Square. John Paul was the first pope from Poland. Later he would be instrumental in the overthrow of atheistic communism in Europe. The attempt on his life happened on the Feast of Our Lady of Fatima. Though he was seriously wounded, the pope's life was spared. He gave credit to Our Lady of Fatima for saving him. In 1983, Pope John Paul II went to the prison to visit and forgive the man who had shot him. Thirty-one years later, after serving twenty-nine years for his crime and converting to Christianity, Ali Agca returned to Rome. He had come to lay flowers on Pope Saint John Paul's grave.

SNAPSHOT

Archbishop Romero

Blessed Óscar Arnulfo Romero y Galdámez (1917–1980) was the archbishop of San Salvador's capital, El Salvador. In 1980 he was killed by an assassin's bullet as he celebrated Mass in a hospital chapel.

The young Óscar was a carpenter's apprentice when he decided to enter the seminary. After his ordination in 1942, he served as a parish priest. Later he became auxiliary bishop of San Salvador and served in a rural diocese. There he witnessed firsthand the sufferings of the poor.

In 1977 Bishop Romero was made the archbishop of San Salvador. This gave him greater opportunity to point out the injustices he saw. At that time many people were being oppressed by the members of the ruling party. Because he spoke out, the archbishop received many threats against his life. His close associate, Father Rutilio Grande, S.J., was murdered. Despite the danger he faced, Romero continued to preach bravely against violence and persecution. In his last homily Archbishop Romero pleaded for peace: "In the name of God, and in the name of this suffering people whose cries rise each day to heaven more urgently, I beg you, I plead with you, I order you in the name of God: Stop the repression!"

Archbishop Oscar Romero is an example to the whole Church of the prophetic Gospel call to justice and peace.

ACTIVITY

If Jesus or our Blessed Mother Mary appeared to you, what would you want to ask? Write a letter to either of them to express your love and trust and to present some situation that needs their attention. Do you think there is something Jesus and Mary might ask *you* to do about this need?

Prayer

Dear God, the end of the second thousand-year period of Christian history has come. How much suffering took place in the last century! There were natural disasters, terrible acts of violence, and too many wars. But at the same time, there was so much progress in fields of science, in inventions, in medicine. How many good people lived in this twentieth century, including members of my own family and many others whom I know. Bless all of us as we try to live together as your children. Amen.

The Bigger Picture

This was the last century of the second millennia of the Christian era. However, when we look at all that took place in that hundred-year period, it seems that it must have been much longer than previous centuries. Great and tragic wars were fought. Grand and loving acts of charity were performed. The twentieth century was a time of extremes in every area of human life.

And yet, looking back on the last hundred years, they seem a bit far away. You weren't even born yet. The new century, the twenty-first century, is *your* century. Before we look at what has happened so far in this new period of Church history, ask yourself what you expect to see as the years go on. What inventions do you expect there will be? Will astronauts establish colonies on other planets? And here on earth, will there be peace? Will all the world's children be able to attend school? Will there be freedom of religious worship so that people can practice their faith without fear? Will the Church be able to overcome any of her divisions? Where will the next pope come from? What changes do you think you might see in your parish?

For Catholics this twenty-first century is a time for new evangelization. Priests and religious are not the only ones who must share the Gospel where it has never been preached. We are all called to be missionaries right where we are. Every one of us can share with others the wonderful story of Jesus Christ and his Church. Whether you know it or not, as a Christian believer today you are already involved in this exciting adventure. How can you prepare for your future and the future of the Church?

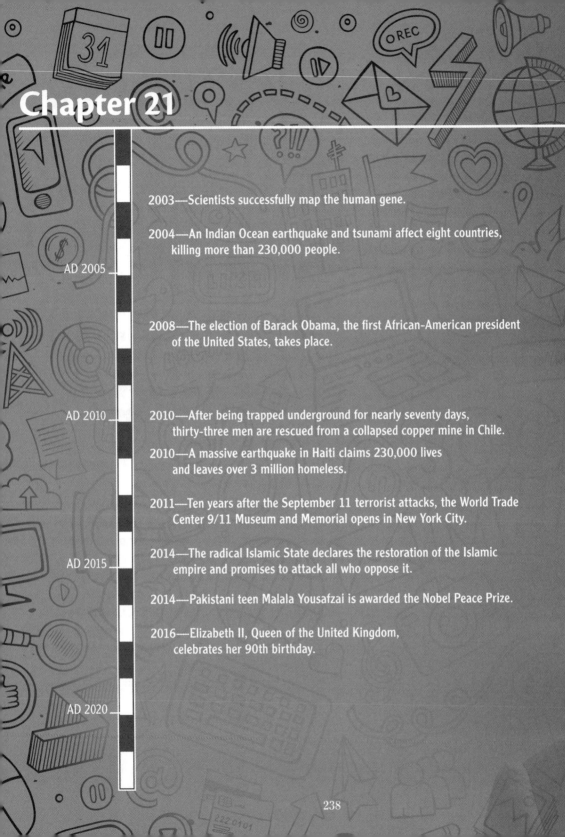

Chapter 21

2003—Scientists successfully map the human gene.

2004—An Indian Ocean earthquake and tsunami affect eight countries, killing more than 230,000 people.

AD 2005

2008—The election of Barack Obama, the first African-American president of the United States, takes place.

AD 2010

2010—After being trapped underground for nearly seventy days, thirty-three men are rescued from a collapsed copper mine in Chile.

2010—A massive earthquake in Haiti claims 230,000 lives and leaves over 3 million homeless.

2011—Ten years after the September 11 terrorist attacks, the World Trade Center 9/11 Museum and Memorial opens in New York City.

2014—The radical Islamic State declares the restoration of the Islamic empire and promises to attack all who oppose it.

AD 2015

2014—Pakistani teen Malala Yousafzai is awarded the Nobel Peace Prize.

2016—Elizabeth II, Queen of the United Kingdom, celebrates her 90th birthday.

AD 2020

Time of New Evangelization

Pope Saint John Paul II

Pope Benedict XVI

Pope Francis

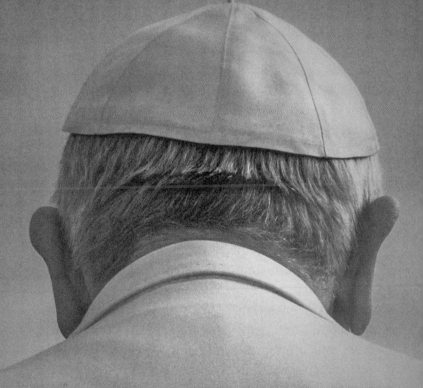

Pope Saint John Paul II

Pope John Paul II helped the Church prepare for the third millennium. A Great Jubilee was to take place from the year 2000 to the year 2001. The pope called for a jubilee to celebrate the two-thousandth anniversary of the birth of Jesus Christ. With it, John Paul hoped that a new era of holiness would begin.

Unfortunately, serious corruption and scandal also came to light in the first years of this century. It became known that some members of the clergy had secretly abused children in the past. This betrayal of trust hurt numerous families. It damaged the respect many of the faithful had for the Church. The Church was struck with sorrow over failing to protect children as she should have. She has since repented of all wrongdoing. She has also made an effort to support the victims and punish those guilty of abuse. Lastly, the Church has taken needed steps to prevent these terrible crimes from ever happening again.

The crisis in the Church took place around the same time as the terrorist attacks of September 11, 2001. These were committed on U.S. soil by the radical Islamist group Al Qaeda. The optimism and promise of the new millennium faded quickly. For many people the world—and even the Church—no longer seemed like safe places.

John Paul II

21st century

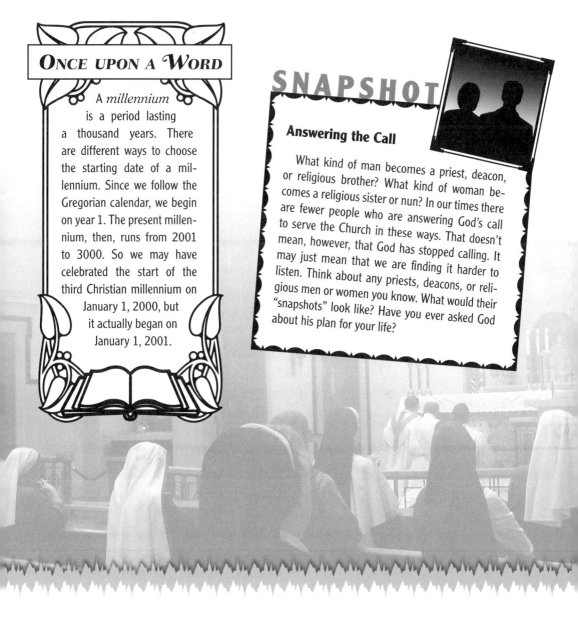

ONCE UPON A *WORD*

A *millennium* is a period lasting a thousand years. There are different ways to choose the starting date of a millennium. Since we follow the Gregorian calendar, we begin on year 1. The present millennium, then, runs from 2001 to 3000. So we may have celebrated the start of the third Christian millennium on January 1, 2000, but it actually began on January 1, 2001.

SNAPSHOT

Answering the Call

What kind of man becomes a priest, deacon, or religious brother? What kind of woman becomes a religious sister or nun? In our times there are fewer people who are answering God's call to serve the Church in these ways. That doesn't mean, however, that God has stopped calling. It may just mean that we are finding it harder to listen. Think about any priests, deacons, or religious men or women you know. What would their "snapshots" look like? Have you ever asked God about his plan for your life?

finish the face

Write your own "I Witness." You are the eyewitness today. What will you say to future generations about life in the twenty-first century?

I Witness

Benedict XVI

Pope Benedict XVI

It soon became evident that Pope John Paul II was gravely ill with Parkinson's disease. On April 2, 2005 he died. The College of Cardinals elected Joseph Ratzinger as the next pope. He was the German cardinal who had worked closely with Pope John Paul II for many years.

The new pope took the name Benedict XVI. The first thing he tried to do was revive faith throughout Europe. The practice of religion had greatly declined over the years. In 2007 Pope Benedict gave permission for churches to celebrate the Tridentine Mass—the Mass of the Council of Trent—in Latin. He did this to help heal divisions that had started with Vatican II. Some Catholics were not comfortable with the changes in the Church's customs and practices after the council. The *Extraordinary Form* of the Mass allowed these people to practice their faith in a more traditional way.

Next Pope Benedict reached out to members of the Church of England. He wanted to help those trying to come into communion with the Catholic Church. The Anglican Ordinariate was created for this purpose. In the Ordinariate English Christian traditions are welcomed, preserved, and shared. Pope Benedict also worked to promote unity between Catholics and Lutherans.

Pope Benedict was a shy man by nature. But he happily continued to invite young people to celebrate World Youth Days. (Pope John Paul II had first started World Youth Day when he was pope.) Benedict also directed the largest beatification in the history of the Church. He beatified some 498 martyrs of the Spanish Civil War (1936–1939). Over and over again Pope Benedict tried to lead people to live in peace. He and Muslim leader Mahdi Mostafavi signed a joint statement in 2008; it affirmed that religion and violence cannot exist together.

Pope Benedict was the first pope to open a social media account. He wanted to stay connected with the faithful, especially with young people. But in February 2013, Pope Benedict surprised the whole Church by making a very rare decision. He resigned from the papacy. Benedict said that the Church needed a younger and more energetic leader. After he stepped down, Pope Benedict XVI retired to a monastery on the Vatican grounds. There he continues to write and to pray. He is referred to as pope emeritus and likes to be called Father Benedict.

On the Record

"I should stay! How can I leave the Christians alone?"

Bishop Giovanni Martinelli spoke these words during a television interview. He is the apostolic vicar of Tripoli. The bishop was referring to the threat of the Islamic State to invade the capitol of Libya and put the Christians to death. When the bishop spoke these words, twenty-one Coptic Christians had been kidnapped and killed simply because they were Christians. They are just a few of the martyrs of today. Bishop Martinelli said that all of us are called to be witnesses for the faith. The whole human family must work diligently for unity instead of seeking our own interests.

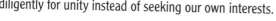

SOCIAL MEDIA

LATEST & GREATEST

It is hard to guess what the most important discovery or invention of the twenty-first century will be. All of our technology is becoming smaller, faster, and more powerful. What do you imagine will be the most important invention we will see this century?

More than the Facts

Scientists are serious about plans to set up a colony on Mars. Perhaps this will become a reality within the century. Potential colonists are currently being trained. They are learning to live in conditions that are similar to those on the Red Planet.

Think of all the challenges the mission to Mars presents. First of all, a spacecraft needs to be built. It must be able to withstand the trip and protect the astronauts and their supplies from the dangers in the Martian atmosphere. Materials need to be designed to help colonists build, produce food, and find water and oxygen sources. But the biggest challenge to setting up a Mars colony is that it will probably be a permanent assignment. Because it is so far away, there may be no way to return to earth. How could this affect those who go? How important do you think a person's faith would have to be for such a trip?

Pope Francis

The news that Pope Benedict was going to retire was followed by another surprise. In March of 2013 the College of Cardinals announced a successor to the pope. They had elected Cardinal Jorge Bergoglio of Argentina. He was the first Latin American and the first Jesuit to be pope. He was also the first pope to choose the name Francis. Finally, he was the first pope to meet with the patriarch of the Russian Orthodox Church to talk about the possibilities for unity.

Pope Francis has been called "the people's pope." Everything he says and does is to bring Jesus and his Church close to people. Francis speaks simply and directly; he never shies away from difficult topics. His actions speak loudly, too. Francis chose to live in a Vatican City hotel rather than the papal apartment. He wanted to set an example of simple living; he also wanted to live in community.

In 2014 Pope Francis called for a synod of bishops from around the world. He wanted them to address some of the biggest challenges that families face today. In the same year Pope Francis declared Pope John XXIII and Pope John Paul II saints. The following year Francis declared an Extraordinary Jubilee Year dedicated to Mercy. Over and over, through his life and words, Pope Francis shows the Church how to approach people with humility and love.

Francis

Mystery of History

Perhaps the most mysterious thing about history is how—and when—it will end. As Christians, we believe that Jesus, the Son of God, will come again. He will not come to earth as a helpless baby the way he did the first time. Instead, he will return in glory and power. When Jesus comes, history as we know it will end, and life in eternity will begin. No one knows when this will occur. In fact, the Bible tells us that "the day and hour no one knows, neither the angels of heaven, nor the Son, but only the Father" (Matt 24:26). That is why we should try to make good use of the time we have here and now. We can do this by doing our best to love God and the people around us.

ACTIVITY

This is a history book, and history is ongoing. Every day a big or little event happens and then immediately passes into history. In a notebook make a record of those events that you believe should be remembered as part of our history.

Prayer

Dear Lord, as I grow up in this century teach me to look for ways to use all that science, technology, language, and the arts offer to praise and serve you. Guide me also to use all of my talents, my intelligence, my opportunities, my education, and all of your gifts of grace to make this life better for my family, my friends, and all the people I will meet. And teach me how to live my faith and share it with others.
Amen.

The Bigger Picture

The bigger picture of the twenty-first century remains a mystery for now. The only thing we know for sure is that we will be part of it. You especially will see this century unfold throughout your lifetime. May every one of us be alert to the opportunities for doing good. May we help to make this century the best in all of the Church's history.

Index

Visit www.pauline.org/churchrocks to download the appendices: Table of Popes, of Church Councils, and of Heresies

Credits

Beck: *Kristina*, 1650, Nationalmuseum, public domain; Wolfgang Hartmann-*View over Stockholm from the east*, 1650, User:Koyos/Wikimedia Commons/Public Domain; ©Ralph Hammann/Wikimedia Commons/CC-BY-SA-4.0; ©User:GFreihalter/Wikimedia Commons/CC-BY-SA-3.0; LACMA/Wikimedia Commons/Public Domain; **page 192**, Art from *Political History of Poland* by E.H. Lewinski-Corwin, 1917/Wikimedia Commons/Public Domain; Louis Caravaque-*Каравак, Луи Портрет Петра I*/Wikimedia Commons/Public Domain; Ustad Mansur/Wikimedia Commons/Public Domain; Joris Joostensz Laerle/Wikimedia Commons/Public Domain; **page 193**, Adriaan Schoonebeek-*Capture of Azov*/Wikimedia Commons/Public Domain; **Chapter 18—page 194**, ©Bernard Gagnon/Wikimedia Commons/CC-BY-SA-3.0; Art from *The Spanish in the Southwest* by Rosa V. Winterburn (New York, Cincinnati: American Book Company, 1903)/Retrieved December 27, 2018 from https://archive.org/stream/spanishinsouthw00wint/spanishinsouthw00wint#page/106/mode/2up; **page 194–195**, Domenick D'Andrea/Wikimedia Commons/Public Domain; **page 195**, Art from *Historical Epochs of the French Revolution* by H. Goudemetz, Project Gutenberg/Wikimedia Commons/Public Domain; **page 196**, ©User:Gisling/Wikimedia Commons/CC-BY-SA-3.0; Johann Matthias-*1744 Homann Heirs Map of Asia*, HaseGeographicus Rare Antique Maps/Wikimedia Commons/Public Domain; Philippe Behagle-*Jesuit astronomers with Kangxi Emperor*/Wikimedia Commons/Public Domain; **page 197**, Christoph Weigel after Caspar Luyken-*Clemens XI* from *Neu-eröffnete Welt-Galleria* (Nürnberg, 1703)/Wikimedia Commons/Public Domain; Antony van der Does-*Portrait of Cornelius Jansenius*, published by Rombout van de Velde, Rijksmuseum/Wikimedia Commons/Public Domain; *Chasuble*, LACMA/Wikimedia Commons/Public Domain; Jean-Baptiste Greuze-*Mozart*/Yale University Art Gallery/public domain; **page 198–199**, Vincenzo Coronelli-*La Louisiana* from *Atlante Veneto* by Vincento Coronelli, 1695, Geographicus Rare Antique Maps/Wikimedia Commons/Public Domain; **page 198**, Arthur C. Haskell, Library of Congress, Historic American Buildings Survey of Massachusetts 075769pv/Wikimedia Commons/Public Domain; User:Naggie34/Wikimedia Commons/Public Domain; ©Edward Wood aka. Elephantwood/Wikimedia Commons/CC-BY-SA-3.0; Unknown-*Portrait of Bartolomeo Cristofori*/Wikimedia Commons/Public Domain; Bartolommeo Cristofori-*Piano e Forte* from *Encyclopædia Britannica*, 11th ed., Vol. 21/Wikimedia Commons/Public Domain; **page 199**, Piaget-van Ravenswaay Collection, Library of Congress, Prints & Photographs Division, MO-1621/Wikimedia Commons/Public Domain; Jack E. Boucher, Library of Congress, Prints & Photographs Division, MO-1105/Wikimedia Commons/Public Domain; Piaget-van Ravenswaay Collection, Library of Congress, Prints & Photographs Division, MO, 97-SAIGEN, 1A-2/Wikimedia Commons/Public Domain; **page 200**, Ferris, Jean Leon Gerome, Artist. *Writing the Declaration of Independence, 1776*/J.L.G. Ferris. , ca. 1932. Cleveland, Ohio: The Foundation Press, Inc., July 28. Photograph. Retrieved from the Library of Congress, https://www.loc.gov/item/2002719535/. (Accessed September 15, 2017); Ferris, Jean Leon Gerome, Artist. *Betsy Ross, 1777*/J.L.G. Ferris. , ca. 1932. Cleveland, Ohio: The Foundation Press, Inc., July 28. Photograph. Retrieved from the Library of Congress, https://www.loc.gov/item/2002719536/. (Accessed October 20, 2017.); Gilbert Stuart-*Portrait of Commodore John Barr*y, by V. Zveg/Wikimedia Commons/Public Domain; Art from *Commodore Joshua Barney* by William Frederick Adams (Springfield, Mass: Priv. print, 1912)/Internet Archive Book Images/Wikimedia Commons/Public Domain; **page ix, 201**, François Séraphin Delpech-*Portrait de Marie Joseph du Motier, marquis de La Fayette*/Wikimedia Commons/Public Domain; **page 201**, Charles Willson Peale-*Louis Lebègue Duportail*/Wikimedia Commons/Public Domain; Art from *La Pologne historique, littéraire, monumentale et illustrée* by Jakób Leonard Chodźko, 1839, British Library, Mechanical Curator collection/Wikimedia Commons/Public Domain; Unknown-*Thomas Fitzsimons*/Wikimedia Commons/Public Domain; http://whenwashingtonwasirish.blogspot.com/2010/11/col-john-fitzgerald.html; Unknown-*Daniel Carroll*/Wikimedia Commons/Public Domain; **page 200–201**, User:Makaristos/Wikimedia Commons/Public Domain; **page 202**, *George Washington* Gift of William H. Huntington, 1883, Metropolitan Museum of Art/Wikimedia Commons/CC0 1.0; Pompeo Batoni-*Ritratto di Pio VI*, ©User:Sailko/Wikimedia Commons/CC-BY-3.0; *Benjamin Franklin*. 1868. Photograph. Retrieved from the Library of Congress, https://www.loc.gov/item/2004671903/. (Accessed January 12, 2018); Gilbert Stuart-*Portrait of Bishop John Carroll*/Wikimedia Commons/Public Domain; **page 203**, ©User:MARELBU/Wikimedia Commons/CC-BY-3.0; Art from *History of the City of New York* by, David Thomas Valentine (New York: G. P. Putnam & Co., 1853)/Retrieved December 27, 2018 from https://archive.org/stream/historyofcityofn00vale_0#page/n315/mode/2up; **page iii, 203**, *Pierre Toussaint*/Wikimedia Commons/Public Domain; **page viii, 203**, ©Burkhard Mücke/Wikimedia Commons/CC-BY-SA-4.0; **page 204**, *Alb Cuff*, LACMA/Wikimedia Commons/Public Domain; Unknown-*Benedict (Baruch) Spinoza*/Wikimedia Commons/Public Domain; Wellcome Library, London. Wellcome Images images@wellcome.ac.uk http://wellcomeimages.org René Descartes. Line engraving by N. Habert, 1697, after F. Hals, 1649. 1697 By: Frans Halsafter: N. HabertPublished/Wikimedia Commons/CC-BY-4.0; Adam Frans van der Meulen-*Louis XIV before Strasbourg*, ©User:Rama/Wikimedia Commons/CC-BY-SA 2.0 FR; herausgegeben von P. Ermini, Nr.682-*Voltaire*/Wikimedia Commons/Public Domain; Wellcome Library, London. Wellcome Images images@wellcome.ac.uk http://wellcomeimages.org Jean-Jacques Rousseau. Stipple engraving by R. Hart after M. Q. de La Tour. Published/Wikimedia Commons/CC-BY-4.0; **page 205**, *Brazil 18th c. JesuitFather*/Wikimedia Commons/Public Domain; Art from *Galerie illustrée de la Compagnie de Jésus* by Alfred HAMY, 1893, User:Grentidez/Wikimedia Commons/Public Domain; User:Esejotas/Wikimedia Commons/Public Domain; **page viii–ix, 206**, Hubert Robert-*Démolition de l'église Saint-Jean-en-Grève*, HaguardDuNord/Wikimedia Commons/Public Domain; **page 206**, User:Tangopaso/Wikimedia Commons/Public Domain; Art from *The Great Controversy between Christ and Satan during the Christian Dispensation* by Ellen Gould Harmon White (Oakland, Cal., New York (etc.): Pacific press publishing company, 1888)/Internet Archive Book Images/Wikimedia Commons/Public Domain; **page 207**, Jacques-Louis David-*Portrait of General Napoleon Bonaparte*, ©Zenodot Verlagsgesellschaft GmbH-Direct Media-Yorck Project/Wikimedia Commons/GFDL*; ©User:Parisette/Wikimedia Commons/CC-BY-SA-3.0; **Chapter 19—page 208–209, 215**, *Ironworks of Dillingen in 1850*/Wikimedia Commons/Public Domain; **page 208**, Johann E. Hahn-*Couple in Wien*, Stanisław Grodyński/Wikimedia Commons/Public Domain; **page 208, 215**, *Bild Maschinenhalle Escher Wyss 1875*/Wikimedia Commons/Public Domain; **page 209, 217**, *Early Irish Immigrants*/Wikimedia Commons/Public Domain; **page 209, 213**, Art by Léon Benett from *The Steam House* by Jules Verne, 1880/Wikimedia Commons/Public Domain; **page 209**, *Britton & Rey, Lithographer. [Miners panning for gold; entering a mine shaft; miners with equipment; and miners cooking at camp/Lith. of Britton & Rey, California St. corn. Montgomery St., S. Francisco]*. California, . [San Francisco: Lithography of Britton & Rey, California Street corner Montgomery Street, 185] Photograph. Retrieved from the Library of Congress, https://www.loc.gov/item/2011661853/. (Accessed December 29, 2017); ©Fabio Alessandro Locati/Wikimedia Commons/CC-BY-SA-3.0; **page 210**, Wellcome Library, London. Wellcome Images images@wellcome.ac.uk http://wellcomeimages.org *Portrait of Louis Pasteur in his laboratory using a microscope.* Wood engraving By: Adrian Mare The Graphic Published: 21 November 1885/Wikimedia Commons/CC-BY-4.0; Art from *Popular Science Monthly Volume 9*, 1876/Wikimedia Commons/Public Domain; Art from *Popular Science Monthly Volume 45*, May 1894/Wikimedia Commons/Public Domain; *Louis Pasteur* CIPC0023©Bibliothèque interuniversitaire de santé/Wikimedia Commons/Licence ouverte; James F. Gibson-*Savage Station, Va. Field hospital after the battle of June 27, 1862*/Library of Congress, Prints & Photographs Division, cwpb.01063/Wikimedia Commons/Public Domain; **page iii, ix, 210**, A.H. Ritchie-*Mary Ann Bickerdyke*, from *Woman's Work in the Civil War* by Linus Pierpont Brockett and Mary C. Vaughan, Project Gutenberg EBook/Wikimedia Commons/Public Domain; **page 211**, User:Prolineserver/Wikimedia Commons/Public Domain; Wellcome Collection https://wellcomecollection.org/works/kt3468qk?query=Gregor+Mendel. *Life of Mendel* by Hugo Iltis, translated by Eden and Cedar Paul, London: Allen & Unwin, 1932/Wikimedia Commons/CC-BY-4.0; ©Martin Stübler/Wikimedia Commons/CC-BY-SA-4.0; **page 212**, Art from *A life of Napoleon Boneparte* by Ida M. Tarbell (New York: McClure, Phillips & co., 1901)/Internet Archive Book Images/Wikimedia Commons/Public Domain; Wilhelm Kuntzemüller/Wikimedia Commons/Public Domain; W. & D. Downey-*Queen Victoria photographed for her Diamond Jubilee, 1897*/Wikimedia Commons/Public Domain; M. Helff, Digital Library of Slovenia 2RLBFC6H/Wikimedia Commons/Public Domain; **page 213**, Unknown-*Bluefields on the Mosquito Coast*/Wikimedia Commons/Public Domain; Unknown-*Victor Emmanuel II of Italy*/Wikimedia Commons/Public Domain; Unknown-*Pope Pius IX*, Library of Congress, Prints & Photographs Division, cph.3b21214/Wikimedia Commons/Public Domain; User:Karelj/Wikimedia Commons/Public Domain; CIA World Factbook/Wikimedia Commons/Public Domain; **page 214**, Ignote, Licence Art Libre/Wikimedia Commons/Free Art License 1.3; Art from *Almanaque Enciclopédico Español Ilustrado para 1871*/Wikimedia Commons/Public Domain; Unknown-*Secondo Pia*/Wikimedia Commons/Public Domain; **page 215**, Karl Benzinger/Wikimedia Commons/Public Domain; **page 216**, Unknown-*Simón Bolívar*/Wikimedia Commons/Public Domain; Cummings & Hilliard-*South America 1821*/Wikimedia Commons/Public Domain; Jacques Reich-*Elizabeth Ann Seton* from *Appletons' Cyclopædia of American Biography, v. 5, p. 465*, 1900/Wikimedia Commons/Public Domain; ©User:Acroterion/Wikimedia Commons/CC-BY-SA-3.0; **page 217**, *North America 1850*, Geographicus Rare Antique Maps/Wikimedia Commons/Public Domain; *The Irish Brigade* by Geo. F. Bristow and B. O'Connor (New York: John J. Daly, 1864), Library of Congress, Notated Music/Wikimedia Commons/Public Domain; *Irish Brigade Chaplains c. 1862*, Library of Congress, Prints & Photographs Division, cwpb.00280/Wikimedia Commons/Public Domain; ©User:Daderot/Wikimedia Commons/CC0 1.0; **page 218**, *Bear Paw Battlefield in Montana*, National Park Service/Wikimedia Commons/Public Domain; F. M. Sargent-*Chief Joseph and family*, ©Washington State Historical Society/Wikimedia Commons/used with permission; *Chief Joseph's Band*, ©Northwest Museum of Arts and Culture/Wikimedia Commons/used with permission; **page iii, ix, 218**, John H. Fouch-*Chief Joseph 3 weeks after surrender*, ©National Anthropological Archives: Smithsonian Institution NAA INV 10000104/Wikimedia Commons/used with permission; **page iii, 219**, S. Polak-*Le Père Damien*, Congregation of the Sacred Hearts of Jesus and Mary; **page 219**, Library of Congress, Prints & Photographs Division, cph.3c03862/Wikimedia Commons/Public Domain; *Thérèse of Lisieux*, ©Archives of Carmel de Lisieux/Wikimedia Commons/used with permission; Unspecified-*Don Bosco a Torino in 1880*/Wikimedia Commons/Public Domain; Image from *The Venerable Don Bosco* by M. S. Pine, 1916/Wikimedia Commons/Public Domain; **page ix, 219**, Unknown-*Saint Katharine Drexel*/Wikimedia Commons/Public Domain; **page 220**, Image from

Les Missionnaires franÁais chasseurs de plantes, http://www.rhododendron.fr/articles/article19d.pdf; Image from *Mostly Mammals* by Richard Lydekker, 1903/ Wikimedia Commons/Public Domain; Image from *Curtis's Botanical Magazine, London vol. 138* by Matilda Smith, J.N.Fitch, lith/Wikimedia Commons/Public Domain; Jane Fortescue Seymour-*Portrait drawing of the very Rev. John Henry Newman* from *Great Testimony Against Scientific Cruelty* by Stephen Coleridge (London: John Lane The Bodley Head. New York: John Lane Company MCMXVIII, 1918) Retrieved from Project Gutenberg eBook #26072, scanned by David Price/Wikimedia Commons/Public Domain; *Saint Catherine Labouré*, Courtesy, Daughters of Charity Province of St. Louise, St. Louis, MO/Wikimedia Commons/used with permission; User:Vassil/Wikimedia Commons/Public Domain; **page iii, 220**, Unknown-*Bernadette Soubirous*/Wikimedia Commons/Public Domain; **page 221**, User:Vassil/Wikimedia Commons/Public Domain; **Chapter 20—page 222**, NASA-*Apollo 11 Mission image, Astronaut Edwin Aldrin walks near the Lunar Module*, 1969–07–20. ID: AS11–40–5903/Wikimedia Commons/Public Domain; Bain News Service, Publisher. *German Prisoners Lined up for Examination.*, 1917. [June 8] Photograph. Retrieved from the Library of Congress, https://www.loc.gov/item/ggb2006000300/. (Accessed December 30, 2017); **page 222–223**, ©User:svc180/Wikimedia Commons/CC-BY-SA-4.0; **page 223, 230, 240, 241**, Stap/Wikimedia Commons/Public Domain; **page 224**, Food Adm., *World War I: Mrs. James Lee Laidlow.* , None. [Between 1910 and 1920] Photograph. Retrieved from the Library of Congress, https://www.loc.gov/item/npc2008011202/. (Accessed December 30, 2017); *Maria Skłodowska-Curie Medallion*, Starwarsbuffyccg at English Wikipedia/FAL.; L0000655 *Sir Alexander Fleming.* Wellcome Library, London. Wellcome Images images@wellcome.ac.uk http://wellcomeimages.org Sir Alexander Fleming. Published/Wikimedia Commons/CC BY 4.0; Unknown-*Workers on the first moving assembly line put together magnetos and flywheels for 1913 Ford autos, Highland Park, Michigan*/Wikimedia Commons/ Public Domain; **page 225**, Giuseppe Felici-*Pope Pius X*/Wikimedia Commons/Public Domain; U.S. Navy-*F4U Corsairs at Lambert Field*/Wikimedia Commons/ Public Domain; **page 226**, *Our Lady of Fatima*-Courtesy of Paulinas Editora, Lisboa, Portugal; **page 226–227**, Department of the Navy. Fourteenth Naval District. 1916–9/18/1947, Photographer-*USSArizona PearlHarbor*, National Archives and Records Administration/Wikimedia Commons/Public Domain; **page 227**, Lewis W. Hine-*Great Depression*, Franklin D. Roosevelt Presidential Library and Museum/Wikimedia Commons/Public Domain; **page 228–229**, *Members of the Royal 22e Regiment in audience with Pope Pius XII*. Canada. Dept. of National Defence/Library and Archives Canada/PA-166069/Wikimedia Commons/Public Domain; **page 229**, *Maksymilian Kolbe*, ©User: Aw58/Wikimedia Commons/CC-BY-SA-3.0 PL; Unknown-*Edith Stein*, The Order of the Carmelites/Wikimedia Commons/ Used with permission; **page 231**, Titian-*Assumption of Mary*, ©Zenodot Verlagsgesellschaft GmbH-Direct Media-Yorck Project/Wikimedia Commons/GFDL*; **page 232**, Bain News Service, Publisher. *Russian Peasants.*, ca. 1915. [Between and Ca. 1920] Photograph. Retrieved from the Library of Congress, https://www. loc.gov/item/ggb2005024231/. (Accessed December 30, 2017); **page 233**, Lothar Wolleh-*Second Vatican Council*/Wikimedia Commons/CC-BY-SA-3.0; **page 234**, Photo by unrecorded photographer on Unsplash (We apologize to the photographer for omitting your name. We could not find it after the image was downloaded.); **page 235**, NASA-*Astronaut Neil A. Armstrong*/NASA on The Commons@Flickr Commons/Public Domain; Frank Hoffman/Department of Energy Oak Ridge-*Exhibit at American Museum of Science and Energy Oak Ridge*/Wikimedia Commons/Public Domain; **page 236**, ProhibitOnions at English Wikipedia/ Wikimedia Commons/Public Domain; Arzobispado de San Salvador; Congregatio de Causis Sanctorum-*Óscar Arnulfo Romero y Galdámez* in 1978/Wikimedia Commons/Public Domain; Photo retrieved March 10, 2017/eCatholic Stock Photos. http://photos.ecatholic.com/gallery/freestockphotos/ photo/231518011; **page 237**, Photo by unrecorded photographer on Unsplash (We apologize to the photographer for omitting your name. We could not find it after the image was downloaded.); **Chapter 21—page 238, 242–243, 244**, ©iStock.com/kostenkodesign; **page 239**, Photo by Nacho Arteaga on Unsplash; **page iii, 240**, ©Daughters of Saint Paul; **page 241**, ©Daughters of Saint Paul/Putri Magadalena Mamesah, FSP; **page 242**, ©Daughters of Saint Paul; **page 243**, ©Marco Verch/ Wikimedia Commons/CC BY 2.0; **page 244**, Photo by NASA on Unsplash; **page 245**, ©Daughters of Saint Paul/Julie Benedicta Marie Turner, FSP; **page 246**, Photo by Joshua Davis on Unslpash; **page 247**, Photo by Josh Applegate on Unsplash

Unless otherwise noted, the last access date for the images was January 12, 2018.

Illustration credits—Jason Bach—page 8, 14, 23, 38, 44, 59, 78, 88, 93, 109, 119, 128, 142, 155, 169, 187, 199, 211, 235, 244;
Mary Joseph Peterson, FSP—page 5, 16, 22, 25, 28, 33, 35, 38, 47, 55, 64, 67, 75, 87, 92, 96, 107, 117, 127, 140, 146, 162, 176, 177, 184, 197, 217, 231

Every effort has been made to trace copyright holders, to obtain their permission for the use of copyrighted material, and attribute such copyright holders herein. The publisher apologizes if there are any errors or omissions. If any permissions have been inadvertently overlooked, the publisher will be pleased to make the necessary and reasonable arrangements at the first opportunity.

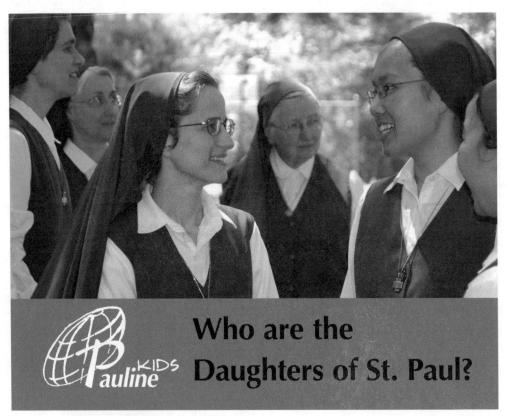

Who are the Daughters of St. Paul?

We are Catholic sisters with a mission. Our task is to bring the love of Jesus to everyone like Saint Paul did. You can find us in over 50 countries. Our founder, Blessed James Alberione, showed us how to reach out to the world through the media. That's why we publish books, make movies and apps, record music, broadcast on radio, perform concerts, help people at our bookstores, visit parishes, host JClub book fairs, use social media and the Internet, and pray for all of you.

Visit our Web site at www.pauline.org

BOOKS & MEDIA

The Daughters of St. Paul operate book and media centers at the following addresses. Visit, call, or write the one nearest you today, or find us at www.paulinestore.org.

CALIFORNIA
3908 Sepulveda Blvd, Culver City, CA 90230 — 310-397-8676
3250 Middlefield Road, Menlo Park, CA 94025 — 650-369-4230

FLORIDA
145 SW 107th Avenue, Miami, FL 33174 — 305-559-6715

HAWAII
1143 Bishop Street, Honolulu, HI 96813 — 808-521-2731

ILLINOIS
172 North Michigan Avenue, Chicago, IL 60601 — 312-346-4228

LOUISIANA
4403 Veterans Memorial Blvd, Metairie, LA 70006 — 504-887-7631

MASSACHUSETTS
885 Providence Hwy, Dedham, MA 02026 — 781-326-5385

MISSOURI
9804 Watson Road, St. Louis, MO 63126 — 314-965-3512

NEW YORK
115 E. 29th Street, New York City, NY 10016 — 212-754-1110

SOUTH CAROLINA
243 King Street, Charleston, SC 29401 — 843-577-0175

TEXAS
No book center; for parish exhibits or outreach evangelization, contact: 210-569-0500 or SanAntonio@paulinemedia.com or P.O. Box 761416, San Antonio, TX 78245

VIRGINIA
1025 King Street, Alexandria, VA 22314 — 703-549-3806

CANADA
3022 Dufferin Street, Toronto, ON M6B 3T5 — 416-781-9131

Smile
God loves you